TEEN RIGHTS AND FREEDOMS

Discipline and Punishment

TEEN RIGHTS AND FREEDOMS

Discipline and Punishment

David Haugen and Susan Musser
Book Editors

GREENHAVEN PRESS
A part of Gale, Cengage Learning

GALE
CENGAGE Learning·

Detroit • New York • San Francisco • New Haven, Conn • Waterville, Maine • London

Elizabeth Des Chenes, *Director, Publishing Solutions*

For more information, contact:
Greenhaven Press
27500 Drake Rd.
Farmington Hills, MI 48331-3535
Or you can visit our Internet site at gale.cengage.com.

For product information and technology assistance, contact us at:

Gale Customer Support, 1-800-877-4253.
For permission to use material from this text or product, submit all requests online at www.cengage.com/permissions.

Further permissions questions can be emailed to permissionrequest@cengage.com.

Articles in Greenhaven Press anthologies are often edited for length to meet page requirements. In addition, original titles of these works are changed to clearly present the main thesis and to explicitly indicate the author's opinion. Every effort is made to ensure the Greenhaven Press accurately reflects the original intent of the authors. Every effort has been made to trace the owners of copyrighted material.

Cover Image: © Design Pics Inc./Alamy.

LIBRARY OF CONGRESS CATALOGING-IN-PUBLICATION DATA

Discipline and punishment / David Haugen and Susan Musser, book editors
    p. cm. -- (Teen rights and freedoms)
    Summary: "Discipline and Punishment: Each volume in the series focuses on a different right or freedom and offers an anthology of key essays and articles on that right or freedom and the responsibilities that come with it"-- Provided by publisher.
    Includes bibliographical references and index.
    ISBN 978-0-7377-6401-7 (hardback)
  1. Students--Legal status, laws, etc.--United States. I. Haugen, David M., 1969- II. Musser, Susan.
    KF4159.D57 2012
    344.73'0793--dc23

                                                   2012009232

Printed in the United States of America
1 2 3 4 5 6 7 16 15 14 13 12

Contents

Foreword   1

Introduction   4

Chronology   7

1. **Discipline and Punishment at School: An Overview**   10
   Gale Encyclopedia of Everyday Law

   A law encyclopedia describes both how the concept of
   discipline has evolved in educational settings and the
   modern policies that define its application today.

2. **College Students Attending a State University
   Must Be Granted a Hearing Before Expulsion**   20
   The US Court of Appeals' Decision

   Richard Rives

   The US Court of Appeals finds in 1961 that six students
   expelled from a state university must be afforded due
   process rights in the course of punishment.

3. **College Disciplinary Systems Are a Necessary
   Element of Higher Education**   31
   Edward N. Stoner and Sheldon E. Steinbach

   A lawyer and an education consultant argue that college
   disciplinary systems are essential to providing students
   with quality education and can provide closure on cases
   that the criminal system does not.

4. **College Disciplinary Codes and Approaches
   Should Not Be Legalistic**   40
   Peter F. Lake

A law university director argues that disciplinary systems in higher education have become too legalistic, and universities would be better served by a more individualized reform.

5. **Students Must Be Granted a Hearing Before Being Suspended or Expelled by a School in Accordance with the Fourteenth Amendment**   50
The US Supreme Court's Decision

Byron White

The US Supreme Court finds in 1975 that prior to punishing a student with suspension, the student in question must be given a hearing under the due process clause of the Fourteenth Amendment.

6. **School Expulsion: A Life Sentence?**   60
Sarah Biehl

An attorney maintains that punishing students with suspension or expulsion denies them the right to an education, causes long-lasting harm, and hinders their pursuit of success and happiness.

7. **School Zero Tolerance Policies Are a Legal and Effective Means of Discipline**   70
National School Boards Association

An association of educators argues that schools have the right to enact reasonable zero tolerance policies and that such policies have been effective in reducing violence and other disruptive or threatening behaviors.

8. **School Zero Tolerance Policies Unfairly Criminalize Children**   78
John W. Whitehead

The president of a civil liberties institute asserts that zero tolerance policies are failing schools by ignoring the contexts of specific infractions and criminalizing childish behavior.

9. **Corporal Punishment Administered at School Does Not Constitute Cruel and Unusual Punishment**   85
   The US Supreme Court's Decision

   Lewis F. Powell Jr.

   A US Supreme Court justice writes in 1977 that the administration of corporal punishment by school officials violates neither the eighth nor the fourteenth amendment to the Constitution.

10. **Corporal Punishment Should Be Banned in All Schools**   94

    Laura W. Murphy, Deborah J. Vagins, and Alison Parker

    Representatives from the American Civil Liberties Union and Human Rights Watch testify before Congress as to why the US government should pass legislation outlawing corporal punishment in schools.

11. **The Mother of a Student Who Was Subjected to Corporal Punishment Urges Lawmakers to Outlaw Its Use in Schools**   102
    Personal Narrative

    Linda Pee

    A mother whose daughter was subjected to corporal punishment at school recounts the negative impact of the punishment on her daughter and calls for legislative action to prevent this from happening to other students.

12. **Domestic Violence Laws Do Not Prohibit Parents from Using Corporal Punishment as a Discipline Tool**   107
The State Court of Appeals' Decision

Mark P. Painter

The Ohio Court of Appeals determines in 2003 that domestic violence laws were not enacted to prevent parents from using corporal punishment to discipline their children.

13. **Corporal Punishment Does Not Constitute Child Abuse**   114
The State Supreme Court's Decision

Alan C. Page

The Minnesota Supreme Court rules in 2008 that the actions of a father who paddled his child thirty-six times cannot be termed physical abuse and are legal within Minnesota law.

14. **Sending Teenagers to Boot Camps**   122
Professor's House

A parenting website contends that juvenile boot camps may offer a "last chance" opportunity to instill discipline and respect in the lives of some troubled teens.

15. **Teen Boot Camps Are Ineffective and Dangerous**   128
Maia Szalavitz

A health and science journalist argues that juvenile boot camps are a torture industry that possesses no scientific evidence to back up claims of effectively rehabilitating wayward children.

16. **World Wide Association of Specialty Programs and Schools Sued by Ex-Students Claiming Abuse** 139

Jennifer Dobner

A journalist reports on a lawsuit brought by former students against a string of privately owned rehabilitation institutions for troubled teens. The students allege the facilities were mismanaged and meted out physical and emotional punishment as well as other forms of abuse.

Organizations to Contact 145

For Further Reading 150

Index 153

Foreword

> *"In the truest sense freedom cannot be bestowed, it must be achieved."*
>
> Franklin D. Roosevelt,
> September 16, 1936

The notion of children and teens having rights is a relatively recent development. Early in American history, the head of the household—nearly always the father—exercised complete control over the children in the family. Children were legally considered to be the property of their parents. Over time, this view changed, as society began to acknowledge that children have rights independent of their parents, and that the law should protect young people from exploitation. By the early twentieth century, more and more social reformers focused on the welfare of children, and over the ensuing decades advocates worked to protect them from harm in the workplace, to secure public education for all, and to guarantee fair treatment for youths in the criminal justice system. Throughout the twentieth century, rights for children and teens—and restrictions on those rights—were established by Congress and reinforced by the courts. Today's courts are still defining and clarifying the rights and freedoms of young people, sometimes expanding those rights and sometimes limiting them. Some teen rights are outside the scope of public law and remain in the realm of the family, while still others are determined by school policies.

Each volume in the Teen Rights and Freedoms series focuses on a different right or freedom and offers an anthology of key essays and articles on that right or freedom and the responsibilities that come with it. Material within each volume is drawn from a diverse selection of primary and secondary sources—journals, magazines, newspapers, nonfiction books, organization newsletters, position papers, speeches, and government documents, with a particular emphasis on Supreme Court and lower court decisions. Volumes also include first-person narratives from young people and others involved in teen rights issues, such as parents and educators. The material is selected and arranged to highlight all the major social and legal controversies relating to the right or freedom under discussion. Each selection is preceded by an introduction that provides context and background. In many cases, the essays point to the difference between adult and teen rights, and why this difference exists.

Many of the volumes cover rights guaranteed under the Bill of Rights and how these rights are interpreted and protected in regard to children and teens, including freedom of speech, freedom of the press, due process, and religious rights. The scope of the series also encompasses rights or freedoms, whether real or perceived, relating to the school environment, such as electronic devices, dress, Internet policies, and privacy. Some volumes focus on the home environment, including topics such as parental control and sexuality.

Numerous features are included in each volume of Teen Rights and Freedoms:

- An annotated **table of contents** provides a brief summary of each essay in the volume and highlights court decisions and personal narratives.
- An **introduction** specific to the volume topic gives context for the right or freedom and its impact on daily life.
- A brief **chronology** offers important dates associated with the right or freedom, including landmark court cases.
- **Primary sources**—including personal narratives and court decisions—are among the varied selections in the anthology.
- **Illustrations**—including photographs, charts, graphs, tables, statistics, and maps—are closely tied to the text and chosen to help readers understand key points or concepts.

- An annotated list of **organizations to contact** presents sources of additional information on the topic.
- A **for further reading** section offers a bibliography of books, periodical articles, and Internet sources for further research.
- A comprehensive subject **index** provides access to key people, places, events, and subjects cited in the text.

Each volume of Teen Rights and Freedoms delves deeply into the issues most relevant to the lives of teens: their own rights, freedoms, and responsibilities. With the help of this se ries, students and other readers can explore from many angles the evolution and current expression of rights both historic and contemporary.

Introduction

Corporal punishment of children has been with civilization throughout recorded history. Perhaps to explain its persistence in the West, one need look no further than the Book of Proverbs, in which a rather lengthy anecdote about "correcting" errant sons has passed down through the ages as the abbreviated adage, "Spare the rod and spoil the child." Early advocates of physical punishment—as well as those who continue the practice today—operate under the philosophy that beating or whipping a child instills obedience and warns against the repetition of bad behavior. In a September 13, 1999, article for the conservative website *Insight on the News*, social commentator Walter E. Williams attests that corporal punishment was prevalent both at home and in schools when he was growing up in the United States during the 1940s and 1950s. He claims that such quick and often public displays ensured that children did not disrespect their elders or misbehave without fear of corporal consequences. Dismissing how child experts might respond to this conclusion, Williams states, "The undeniable fact is the 'uncivilized' practice of whipping children produced more civilized young people."

For Williams, the notion of creating "civilized" young people creates a disregard for authority and an excess of will. To Williams, this excess of will often leads to criminal behavior as children progress into adulthood. Historian Benjamin Abelow takes the concept of childhood willfulness and installs it as a cornerstone of religious doctrine. Abelow asserts that many world belief systems speak of corporal punishment as a means to enforce obedience and as a way of purging young people of sin. "Children reared with corporal discipline learn that, to avoid punishment, they must suppress the will and psychologically disengage from aspects of their inner selves that are associated with willfulness," Abelow writes in a chapter of the 2009 anthology *The Biology of Religious Behavior*. He then makes the claim that salvation from punishment—meaning the control of one's will in order to avoid physical punishment—is equated with spiritual "salvation," a goal drilled into new disciples at a very young age. Thus, obedience is a way to escape corporal punishment and a path toward salvation.

The debate about the effectiveness of corporal punishment is not new. Some Enlightenment thinkers believed that beating children did not discourage the willfulness that religious doctrine tried to restrain. In his late seventeenth-century treatise *Some Thoughts Concerning Education*, English philosopher John Locke argued that children can be taught the rationality of controlling their impulses. He maintained that physical punishment—a mark upon the body—left little imprint on the mind. In fact, Locke believed beatings or whippings encouraged children to root their feelings within the flesh rather than learn the reasoning behind right and wrong.

In the eighteenth and nineteenth centuries, social reformers built upon Enlightenment ideals and burgeoning liberal legal scholarship to contend that physical punishment—as Locke proposed—had no lasting effect on children except to understand cruelty. After some noted deaths—including the fatal beating of a thirteen-year-old at the hands of a schoolmaster in England—the ideas of reformers gained traction in the public square. At the turn of the nineteenth century, the most liberal Victorians built upon Romantic-era notions of the idyllic and innocent nature of childhood. Although many English children in Victorian times were slaving at jobs in mines and factories, some social theorists emphasized that childhood should be a time of carefree exploration—a time unconcerned with the weighty issues that would soon enough beset adulthood. However, the Victorian era was also marked by severe repression, and many English households functioned through strict discipline and physical punishment of children to instill proper behavior and pious thoughts. As with most succeeding periods of history, the Victorians navigated conflicting notions of childrearing and the aptness of corporal punishment.

Today, the debate is still prevalent. In a 2002 analysis of several major studies pertaining to the corporal punishment of children, psychologist Elizabeth Gershoff found that researchers drew connections between corporal punishment and ten negative outcomes in children's physical and mental behavior. These included increased aggression, antisocial behavior, and a diminished quality of relationship with parents. The one factor that registered positively was the increased immediate compliance of the child. In her article published in *Psychological Bulletin*, Gershoff writes, "There is general consensus that corporal punishment is effective in getting children to comply immediately while at the same time there is caution from child abuse researchers that corporal punishment by its nature can escalate into physical maltreatment." Despite these findings, an ABC poll conducted in the same year found that 65 percent of US parents approved of spanking as a means of child discipline, while only 31 percent opposed it.

Giving parents final say in the matter of childrearing is still ingrained in the US legal system. Corporal punishment remains legal within all fifty states, and nineteen of those have no law against corporal punishment in state schools (where teachers are assumed to act *in loco parentis*, in place of parents). Globally, nineteen European countries and five others have completely banned corporal punishment at home and at school, but this only represents 12 percent of the world's nations. The notion that government should not intercede in certain aspects of family life remains strong across the majority of the globe, and parental rights still seem to trump children's rights in some arenas.

Teen Rights and Freedoms: Discipline and Punishment examines how children's rights are defined as related to punishment and what constitutes a violation of those rights in the home and at school.

Chronology

1867

New Jersey becomes the first state in the United States to ban corporal punishment in public schools.

August 4, 1961

In *Dixon v. Alabama*, the US Supreme Court finds that, in accordance with their due process rights, college students attending a public university must be given an expulsion hearing before punishment is enacted.

1971

More than a century after New Jersey enacts its ban, Massachusetts becomes the second US state to outlaw corporal punishment in public schools.

January 22, 1975

The US Supreme Court rules in *Goss v. Lopez* that students' due process rights must be observed by public schools when a student is to be suspended.

April 19, 1977

The US Supreme Court rules in *Ingraham v. Wright* that corporal punishment is permissible in public schools and does not constitute cruel and unusual punishment as defined by the Eighth Amendment.

March 1, 1978

In *Board of Curators, University of Missouri v. Horowitz*, the US Supreme Court finds that the Fourteenth Amendment does not require a hearing in circumstances where student expulsion results from poor academic performance.

December 12, 1989   US Congress passes the Drug-Free Schools and Campuses Act of 1989, which creates a federal ban on illegal use, possession, and distribution of drugs and alcohol on school and college grounds and requires schools to enact strict discipline for violation of these rules.

October 24, 1994   The Gun-Free Schools Act of 1994 imposes a mandatory expulsion of at least one year for any student found with a firearm on school campuses, leading to the adoption of zero tolerance firearms and weapons policies at many schools.

March 18, 1998   A US Department of Education survey reveals the prevalence of zero tolerance policies when it reports that around 90 percent of public schools have a zero tolerance policy regarding firearms and other weapons; the majority of schools have zero tolerance for alcohol (87 percent) and drugs (88 percent), and 79 percent observe zero tolerance for violence.

July 18, 2003   A US Court of Appeals judge rules in *State v. Adaranijo* that parents may use corporal punishment as a means of punishing their children, continuing the court's reluctance to intervene into family and home discipline.

August 28, 2007   The US Sixth Circuit Court finds in *Laney v. Farley* that the punishment of in-school suspension does not necessitate the observance of due process or require a suspension hearing.

May 30, 2008   The Minnesota State Supreme Court finds in *In the Matter of the Welfare of the Children of: N.F. and S.F., Parents* that parents' use of corporal punishment to discipline their children does not fall under the definition of child abuse.

June 2010   The US federal government continues to allow states to determine whether corporal punishment in schools should be banned when the US House Committee on Education and Labor declines to vote on a bill that would enact a nationwide ban on the practice in schools.

2011   New Mexico becomes the thirty-first US state to forbid corporal punishment in public schools.

> "Academic codes of conduct aim to
> support educational goals and be in
> line with criminal and civil laws. . . .
> The courts have had the task of
> deciding if the codes achieve this end."

Discipline and Punishment at School: An Overview

Gale Encyclopedia of Everyday Law

The following viewpoint offers an overview of discipline and punishment in the educational system in the United States. The author defines discipline as a concept within schools, showing how educators have, over time, adhered to different philosophies to determine how to manage unruly behavior. The author also reveals how school boards draft codes of conduct to define what is and is not permissible on school grounds. These codes have often been the subject of legal debate, the author states, as lawyers and school boards negotiate how well the rules uphold the aims of discipline within the educational system.

The word, discipline, is akin to the word, disciple. Discipline, in its first definition, means learning, just as the word, disciple, refers to one who learns. Additional meanings of the word, discipline, suggest the complexity of the subject as it pertains to individuals (in this case specifically minors) and the U.S. public school system. Discipline refers to training and experience that corrects, molds, and strengthens individuals' mental faculties and moral character. It also refers to punishment which intends to correct and which is enforced by those in authority or may be self-imposed. Discipline refers to the control gained by enforcing obedience, and it refers to the systematic orderly behavior defined by codes or rules set forth by institutions for their members. Discipline also refers to self-control, to the development of skills that help individuals resist temptation, act positively, and function both independently and cooperatively in ways which enhance personal development and community life. All of these definitions have been central to educators' efforts to find the most effective and useful way to support child development and learning.

Origin of Corporal Punishment

In the colonial era, the Puritan belief that humankind is innately tainted by the Original Sin of Adam and Eve led adults to see children as contaminated by an evil element which needed to be driven out by force. Puritans believed that all disobedience and academic error was the work of Satan, and children's innate proclivity for evil had to be destroyed through pain and humiliation. The idea that suffering corrects became fundamental to institutional design, whether that design was the stocks in which prisoners were displayed for public abuse or the raised stools and dunce caps intended to correct student misbehavior or ignorance through humiliation. "To spare the rod," it was believed, led inevitably to spoiling the child, so slapping, spanking, and whipping were generally understood as beneficial educational tools. These beliefs persisted. Indeed, as late as 1977, in *Ingraham v. Wright*, the U.S. Supreme Court ruled that spanking did not violate students' rights, noting the widespread use of corporal punishment to maintain discipline in educational settings. Corporal punishment remained legal thereafter in over twenty states.

Corporal punishment has long been used for discipline in classrooms, as reflected by this mid-nineteenth-century etching by W.H. Knight. © Time Life Pictures/Mansell/Time Life Pictures/Getty Images.

History of School Discipline

The U.S. Constitution does not address the subject of public education. Apparently the Founding Fathers thought the implementation of schools ought to be the sole responsibility of the states. Initially, education was for the wealthy, and a belief persisted through the eighteenth century that poor individuals were not educable or were not worthy of being educated. In 1852, however, then secretary of state of Massachusetts Horace Mann urged that states be obliged to offer public education to all children. The revolutionary idea behind this plea was that all individuals could and should be educated irrespective of economic class.

During the middle of the nineteenth century, some U.S. educators studied European models, for example, the theories of Philipp Emanuel von Fellenberg (1771–1844) who urged that corporal punishment not be used for academic errors and suggested that learning occurred best with encouragement and kindness. Francis Parker introduced European ideas into the public school system in Quincy, Illinois. What came to be known as the progressive Quincy Movement attached kindergarten to elementary education and extended into the early grades the idea of learning through play. These pedagogical developments examined connections between education and discipline and considered teachers' roles in creating environments conducive to learning.

By 1910 attendance at public school was mandatory; children were thus absent on a daily basis from parental direction and placed under the authority of educators. This transfer extended teachers' roles to parental disciplinarians; teachers functioned *in loco parentis*, meaning in the place of parents. During the first decades of the 1900s as teachers were stepping further into these parental roles, State legal systems were beginning to evolve ways to handle juvenile offenders which intended to distinguish them from adult perpetrators. One value attached to this development asserted that while adults should be punished for their crimes, children should be rehabilitated for theirs, thus formalizing a beginning to the separation between juvenile misconduct and suffering as its remedy.

At the beginning of the twentieth century, good discipline was evinced as students sitting quietly while they learned by rote. The conventional wisdom saw education as a process of controlling student behavior while information was transferred from teacher to student. This model continues to shape concepts about classroom activities and goals. Challenging this model, however, were the increasingly popular post-World War II theories of Benjamin Spock (1903–1998), who disapproved of rigid childrearing techniques and urged adults, parents, and teachers alike, to be more affectionate and flexible. Some critics of Spock's theories asserted that they contributed to a growing attitude of permissiveness and relativity which blurred children's understanding of right and wrong and encouraged self-defeating traits like selfishness, indolence, or noncompliance. Additionally, in the second half of the twentieth century, health-care professionals and educators became more informed about how student misbehavior may be connected to physiological or psychological problems, like attention deficit disorder, hyper-activity, or emotional disturbance. Changes in the family unit, increase in the Hollywood celebration of violence, and effects of illegal drug use also affected students' ability and willingness to learn in school. Finally, in the 1990s, juveniles committed serious felonies on school property, some of which converted schools temporarily to war zones. Reactions to these events caused many people to advocate for a return to more stringent controls of students, which in some circles acquired the label, zero tolerance.

School Boards Draft Codes of Conduct

In taking charge of students and teaching them, twentieth-century educators repeatedly faced the challenge of designing codes of conduct. Doing so required attention to multiple and sometimes seemingly conflicting issues: school organizational needs, the goals of education, and the nebulous area of personal rights both for those in charge and for those being controlled. Educators had to identify features conducive for learning and then set forth rules and consequences for misconduct which would allow problem children to be handled constructively while the behaving majority of students continued to learn with-out disruption. In short, educators had to define ways to support classroom productivity, encourage student academic progress, and bring misbehaving individuals back to positive conduct so they could resume learning. In this task, educators, administrators, and staff became increasingly conscious of legal issues connected to students' rights, juvenile legal status, and the handling of student crime. All of these issues were addressed independently by different school boards across the nation and handled differently by school boards and courts over time.

PERCENTAGE OF STUDENTS AGES 12–18 WHO REPORTED SELECTED SECURITY MEASURES AT SCHOOL				
Security Measure	**2001**	**2003**	**2005**	**2007**
Total	99.4	99.3	99.6	99.8
One or more security cameras to monitor the school	38.5	47.9	57.9	66.0
Security guards and/or assigned police officers	63.6	69.6	68.3	68.8
Other school staff or other adult supervision in the hallway	88.3	90.6	90.1	90.0
A code of student conduct	95.1	95.3	95.5	95.9

Taken from: National Center for Education Statistics, US Department of Education.

Codes of Conduct Adhere to Certain Rules

The issues involved in the process of developing these codes of conduct constitute an important part of pedagogical debate and ongoing courtroom deliberation. For example, in *Blackwell v. Issaquene Co. Board* (5th Cir Miss 373 f2d 749) and *Baker v. Downey Board* (California Dist. Ct 307 F supp517), court decisions attempted to define those school requirements and regulations which a court would deem "reasonable." A properly written document had to meet four criteria in order to carry a legal presumption of validity:

- The rules had to be in writing: Regulations students had to obey without a specific verbal command must be in writing.

- The rules had to be specific: Policies had to be clearly stated to students, and without referring to an outside source or document the rules had to explain what was expected and what was prohibited.
- The writing had to be authorized: The writer of the rules had to have the authority to define them.
- The written rules had to be published: The code of conduct had be printed and distributed, for example in student handbooks, in letters home to parents, in public announcements during class time and assemblies, and in postings on bulletin boards.

Richard Curwin, a professor of Education at San Francisco State University, devised criteria for making codes of conduct more effective. His suggestions were:

- To use positive rather than negative statements
- To be definite about proper and prohibited behavior
- To be brief
- To spell out consequences

Thus, the courts began the process of educating the educators on how to arrange the business of school so that when it responded to misbehavior its rulings would be deemed valid in the legal setting.

Content of Codes

In light of their wisdom, experience, and training, educators devised these codes to meet their schools' particular goals and challenges. Some school codes employed step programs which distinguished first offenders from repeat offenders and which handed down mild penalties for first-offense students but then graduated the penalties for the misconduct of repeat offenders. In these cases, students faced consequences determined by their records of behavior. Thus, for a repeat offender a minor infraction might carry the serious penalty of suspension while the same infraction might elicit only a verbal reminder for the first offender. Some schools set aside special classrooms for extra training in matters of self-control, conflict resolution, and co-operation. Schools elicited parents' participation and support in encouraging their children back to positive behavior and academic progress.

Discipline policies stated clearly that rules benefited everyone in the educational community and were in effect inside school buildings, on school property, inside school-owned vehicles, and at school-sponsored activities on or off campus. Codes included rules about attendance, absence, and tardiness. They outlined steps for parents to take in excusing their children from class and the requirements of teachers in how to keep records of student attendance. Patterns of unexcused absence or tardiness were quantified and carried penalties or repercussions which correlated to the extent of the patterns of absence. Misbehaving students might be detained in the classroom after other students were free to go on to non-classroom activities, or they might be required to attend a Saturday detention period. During these times, students might be given extra academic work or required to perform maintenance chores on school property. Repeat offenders were subject by degrees to removal from school; they were removed from class to a study room; placed in an on-sight suspension area; suspended for a specified time; and expelled. Thus, for the benefit of the majority, those individuals who acted out, arguably the ones most in need of education and support, tended to be increasingly marginalized.

When students break the law on school property, police officers must take over for educators. Students who use alcohol or other drugs, who have in their possession or deliver to others controlled substances, who carry weapons, who assault others, are all subject to the same laws they would face elsewhere in the community. Therefore, these forms of misconduct are not within the school's jurisdiction solely. Students can be charged for crimes committed on school property; they can go to court and face court decisions that place them in juvenile detention centers. Clearly, school codes must address a vast range of conduct and take into consideration innumerable factors that lie in or beyond the education setting. The codes must respond legally, in line with community, state, and federal laws on issues connected to discrimination, harassment, gender, and disability. Academic codes of conduct aim to support educational goals and be in line with criminal and civil laws. Often times the courts have had the task of deciding if the codes achieve this end.

Codes Cannot Infringe on Students' Constitutional Rights

Educators have to negotiate the complicated terrain of competing entities, managing difficult students yet remaining mindful of their constitutional rights, for example, their rights to privacy, just cause, and due process. When crime in schools involves police, certain subjects, conflicts, and events may come before the courts. Courts elucidate legal issues but not once and for all: these judgments can be subsequently redefined, upheld, or found unconstitutional. Questions recur pertaining to the application of Fourteenth Amendment protections to students as these individuals are subjected to school regulations. . . .

Columbine and Its Aftermath: Zero Tolerance

On April 20, 1999 at Columbine High School in Littleton, Colorado, two heavily armed students killed twelve students and one teacher and seriously wounded nearly two dozen others before killing themselves. The following month in Conyers, Georgia, a 15-year-old student wounded six other students. In December an Oklahoma middle-school student took a semi-automatic handgun to school and wounded five students. In March 2001 a California student killed two classmates and wounded thirteen others.

These and other murders perpetrated by children against classmates and teachers caused a furor of reactive security measures, precaution taking, and a new commitment to stringent control. Zero tolerance, which initially referred to students carrying weapons to school, fueled provisions for suspension and expulsion and increased them. In Chicago, in the wake of commitment to zero tolerance, suspensions and expulsions jumped to an average of 90 per week, mostly Latinos and African Americans. Proponents of more stringent codes pointed to the staggering fact that every day in the United States twelve children are killed by gunshot. The fact that one day they were gathered together in their deaths at Columbine brought national consciousness to a new level. Many schools nationwide, particularly in urban settings, instigated entry-area body and bag searches, stricter dress codes, and random drug testing. Yet critics of this stringent disciplinary action urged educators to return to a positive vision of students and search for punishments that teach rather than using those that increase the drop-out rate.

> *"Whenever a governmental body acts so as to injure an individual, the Constitution requires that the act be consonant with due process of law."*

College Students Attending a State University Must Be Granted a Hearing Before Expulsion

The US Court of Appeals' Decision

Richard Rives

On February 25, 1960, students from Alabama State College staged a sit-in at the Montgomery, Alabama, courthouse's basement restaurant after they were denied service; in the following days, they participated in additional demonstrations. In response, the president of the college and the Alabama State Board of Education expelled nine of the involved students without giving notice of the punishment or a disciplinary hearing. Six of the nine expelled students filed a formal complaint in court alleging that the college violated their right to due process. The district court found that the college acted within its legal right to expel the students; however, the Fifth Circuit appeals court ruled that

Richard Rives, Opinion of the Court, *Dixon v. Alabama State Board of Education*, United States Court of Appeals Fifth Circuit, August 4, 1961.

*students attending a public university must be granted due pro-
cess rights in accordance with the Fourteenth Amendment. In the
following viewpoint, Judge Richard Rives finds that the expulsion
deprived the students of their right to an education, and in accordance with previous court decisions, the school, as a public
institution, must observe due process of the law before handing
down such punishment.*

The question presented by the pleadings and evidence, and
decisive of this appeal, is whether due process requires notice and some opportunity for hearing before students at a tax-
supported college are expelled for misconduct. We answer that
question in the affirmative. . . .

Disciplinary Hearings Were
Standard Practice

The evidence clearly shows that the question for decision does
not concern the sufficiency of the notice or the adequacy of the
hearing, but is whether the students had a right to any notice or
hearing whatever before being expelled. The district court wrote
at some length on that question, as appears from its opinion.
After careful study and consideration, we find ourselves unable
to agree with the conclusion of the district court that no notice
or opportunity for any kind of hearing was required before these
students were expelled.

It is true, as the district court said, that "there is no statute
or rule that requires formal charges and/or a hearing," but the
evidence is without dispute that the usual practice at Alabama
State College had been to give a hearing and opportunity to offer defenses before expelling a student. Defendant Trenholm, the
College President, testified:

*Q. The essence of the question was, will you relate to the Court
the usual steps that are taken when a student's conduct has*

developed to the point where it is necessary for the administration to punish him for that conduct?

A. We normally would have conference with the student and notify him that he was being asked to withdraw, and we would indicate why he was being asked to withdraw. That would be applicable to academic reasons, academic deficiency, as well as to any conduct difficulty.

Q. And at this hearing ordinarily that you would set, then the student would have a right to offer whatever defense he may have to the charges that have been brought against him?

A. Yes.

The Due Process Clause Almost Always Applies

Whenever a governmental body acts so as to injure an individual, the Constitution requires that the act be consonant with due process of law. The minimum procedural requirements necessary to satisfy due process depend upon the circumstances and the interests of the parties involved. As stated by Mr. Justice [Felix] Frankfurter concurring in *Joint Anti-Fascist Refugee Committee v. McGrath*, 1951:

> Whether the *ex parte* procedure [in which only one party to the act in question is required to be present] to which the petitioners were subjected duly observed 'the rudiments of fair play,' cannot be tested by mere generalities or sentiments abstractly appealing. The precise nature of the interest that has been adversely affected, the manner in which this was done, the reasons for doing it, the available alternatives to the procedure that was followed, the protection implicit in the office of the functionary whose conduct is challenged, the balance of hurt complained of and good accomplished; these are some of the considerations that must enter into the judicial judgment.

"Once the decision to expel a pupil has been made, the Administration moves quickly," cartoon by Patrick Hardin. www.CartoonStock.com.

Just last month [July 1961], a closely divided Supreme Court held in a case where the governmental power was almost absolute and the private interest was slight that no hearing was required. *Cafeteria and Restaurant Workers Union v. McElroy et al.*, 1961. In that case, a short-order cook working for a privately operated cafeteria on the premises of the Naval Gun Factory in the City of Washington was excluded from the Gun Factory as a security risk. So, too, the due process clause does not require that an alien never admitted to this Country be granted a hearing before being *excluded. United States ex rel. Knauff v. Shaughnessy*, 1950.

In such case the executive power as implemented by Congress to *exclude* aliens is absolute and not subject to the review of any court, unless expressly authorized by Congress. On the other hand, once an alien has been admitted to lawful residence in the United States and remains physically present here it has been held that, "although Congress may prescribe conditions for his expulsion and deportation, not even Congress may expel him without allowing him a fair opportunity to be heard." *Kwong Hai Chew v. Colding*, 1953.

It is not enough to say, as did the district court in the present case, "The right to attend a public college or university is not in and of itself a constitutional right." That argument was emphatically answered by the Supreme Court in the *Cafeteria and Restaurant Workers Union* case, when it said that the question of whether "summarily denying Rachel Brawner access to the site of her former employment violated the requirements of the Due Process Clause of the Fifth Amendment cannot be answered by easy assertion that, because she had no constitutional right to be there in the first place, she was not deprived of liberty or property by the Superintendent's action. 'One may not have a constitutional right to go to Bagdad, but the Government may not prohibit one from going there unless by means consonant with due process of law.'" As in that case, so here, it is necessary to consider "the nature both of the private interest which has been impaired and the governmental power which has been exercised."

Due Process Is Required of Public and Private Organizations

The appellees urge upon us that under a provision of the Board of Education's regulations the appellants waived any right to notice and a hearing before being expelled for misconduct. [This states:]

> Attendance at any college is on the basis of a mutual decision of the student's parents and of the college. Attendance at a par-

ticular college is voluntary and is different from attendance at a public school where the pupil may be required to attend a particular school which is located in the neighborhood or district in which the pupil's family may live. Just as a student may choose to withdraw from a particular college at any time for any personally-determined reason, the college may also at any time decline to continue to accept responsibility for the supervision and service to any student with whom the relationship becomes unpleasant and difficult.

We do not read this provision to clearly indicate an intent on the part of the student to waive notice and a hearing before expulsion. If, however, we should so assume, it nonetheless remains true that the State cannot condition the granting of even a privilege upon the renunciation of the constitutional right to procedural due process. . . . Only private associations have the right to obtain a waiver of notice and hearing before depriving a member of a valuable right. And even here, the right to notice and a hearing is so fundamental to the conduct of our society that the waiver must be clear and explicit. In the absence of such an explicit waiver, Alabama has required that even private associations must provide notice and a hearing before expulsion. In *Medical and Surgical Society of Montgomery County v. Weatherly*, it was held that a physician could not be expelled from a medical society without notice and a hearing. In *Local Union No. 57, etc. v. Boyd*, 1944, a local union was ordered to reinstate one of its members expelled after a hearing of which he had insufficient notice.

The precise nature of the private interest involved in this case is the right to remain at a public institution of higher learning in which the plaintiffs were students in good standing. It requires no argument to demonstrate that education is vital and, indeed, basic to civilized society. Without sufficient education the plaintiffs would not be able to earn an adequate livelihood, to enjoy life to the fullest, or to fulfill as completely as possible the duties and responsibilities of good citizens.

There was no offer to prove that other colleges are open to the plaintiffs. If so, the plaintiffs would nonetheless be injured by the interruption of their course of studies in mid-term. It is most unlikely that a public college would accept a student expelled from another public college of the same state. Indeed, expulsion may well prejudice the student in completing his education at any other institution. Surely no one can question that the right to remain at the college in which the plaintiffs were students in good standing is an interest of extremely great value.

Court Precedents Were Misinterpreted

Turning then to the nature of the governmental power to expel the plaintiffs, it must be conceded, as was held by the district court, that that power is not unlimited and cannot be arbitrarily exercised. Admittedly, there must be some reasonable and constitutional ground for expulsion or the courts would have a duty to require reinstatement. The possibility of arbitrary action is not excluded by the existence of reasonable regulations. There may be arbitrary application of the rule to the facts of a particular case. Indeed, that result is well nigh inevitable when the Board hears only one side of the issue. In the disciplining of college students there are no considerations of immediate danger to the public, or of peril to the national security, which should prevent the Board from exercising at least the fundamental principles of fairness by giving the accused students notice of the charges and an opportunity to be heard in their own defense. Indeed, the example set by the Board in failing so to do, if not corrected by the courts, can well break the spirits of the expelled students and of others familiar with the injustice, and do inestimable harm to their education.

The district court, however, felt that it was governed by precedent, and stated that, "the courts have consistently upheld the validity of regulations that have the effect of reserving to the college the right to dismiss students at any time for any reason without divulging its reason other than its being for the general

Alabama State College students staged a sit-in at the Montgomery, Alabama, courthouse after being denied service at a lunch counter. They were subsequently expelled from their college without notice. © Donald Uhrbrock/Time Life Pictures/Getty Images.

The *In Loco Parentis* Doctrine's Impact Continues

If it is clear that a "state university is without question a state actor," [as defined in *Lugar v. Edmonson Oil Co.*, 1982] why have courts historically been reluctant to weigh in on the procedures employed by universities to discipline students and the outcomes they reach? Why have the courts decided that the full-scale procedural due process requirements characteristic of criminal or civil trials are unnecessary in serious university disciplinary settings? The reasons likely include the history of the educational setting, the historical view of the student, and the evolution of the importance of education within society and the eyes of the court. The university, due in part to its unique history, is treated with greater deference than the State itself with respect to the protections the university must provide under the Fourteenth Amendment.

Arguably, courts of the past were less willing to impose even minimal rules that might hamper the wide discretion universities enjoyed in conducting and deciding university disciplinary hearings because of the applicability of the doctrine of *in loco parentis*. The Latin term *in loco parentis* literally means "to stand in the place of a parent." While the doctrine does not apply directly to the relationship of students and post-secondary institutions today, the great discretion the doctrine afforded universities in the past has certainly left some imprint on the courts of today.

Elizabeth Ledgerwood Pendlay, "Procedure for Pupils: What Constitutes Due Process in a University Disciplinary Hearing?," North Dakota Law Review, vol. 82, no. 3, 2006.

benefit of the institution." With deference, we must hold that the district court has simply misinterpreted the precedents.

The language above quoted from the district court is based upon language found in 14 C.J.S. [*Corpus Juris Secundum,* an encyclopedia of US law] Colleges and Universities § 26, p. 1360, which, in turn, is paraphrased from *Anthony v. Syracuse University*. This case, however, concerns a private university and follows the well-settled rule that the relations between a student and a private university are a matter of contract. The *Anthony* case held that the plaintiffs had specifically waived their rights to notice and hearing. The precedents for public colleges are collected in a recent annotation cited by the district court. We have read all of the cases cited to the point, and we agree with what the annotator himself says: "The cases involving suspension or expulsion of a student from a public college or university all involve the question whether the hearing given to the student was adequate. In every instance the sufficiency of the hearing was upheld." None held that no hearing whatsoever was required. Two cases not found in the annotation have held that some form of hearing is required. In *Commonwealth ex rel. Hill v. McCauley*, 1886, the court went so far as to say that an informal presentation of the charges was insufficient and that a state-supported college must grant a student a full hearing on the charges before expulsion for misconduct. In *Gleason v. University of Minnesota*, 1908 . . . the court held that the plaintiff stated a prima facie ["at first sight"] case upon showing that he had been expelled without a hearing for alleged insufficiency in work and acts of insubordination against the faculty.

The appellees rely also upon *Lucy v. Adams*, 1957, where Autherine Lucy was expelled from the University of Alabama without notice or hearing. That case, however, is not in point. Autherine Lucy did not raise the issue of an absence of notice or hearing.

Due Process Is a Fundamental Right

It was not a case denying any hearing whatsoever but one passing upon the adequacy of the hearing [*People ex rel. Bluett v. Board of Trustees of University of Illinois*], which provoked from Professor Warren A. Seavey of Harvard the eloquent comment:

> At this time when many are worried about dismissal from public service, when only because of the overriding need to protect the public safety is the identity of informers kept secret, when

we proudly contrast the full hearings before our courts with those in the benighted countries which have no due process protection, when many of our courts are so careful in the protection of those charged with crimes that they will not permit the use of evidence illegally obtained, our sense of justice should be outraged by denial to students of the normal safeguards. It is shocking that the officials of a state educational institution, which can function properly only if our freedoms are preserved, should not understand the elementary principles of fair play. It is equally shocking to find that a court supports them in denying to a student the protection given to a pickpocket.

We are confident that precedent as well as a most fundamental constitutional principle support our holding that due process requires notice and some opportunity for hearing before a student at a tax-supported college is expelled for misconduct.

> *"Leaving conduct that may violate both criminal law and college standards solely in the hands of the local police would guarantee a horrible result."*

College Disciplinary Systems Are a Necessary Element of Higher Education

Edward N. Stoner and Sheldon E. Steinbach

In the following viewpoint, Edward N. Stoner and Sheldon E. Steinbach respond to critics who claim that universities fail to adequately punish individuals for crimes committed on campus, particularly sexual violence. Stoner and Steinbach contend that the preliminary counseling and confidential nature of college proceedings provide victims with security not available in the criminal court setting, which when combined with swift action and more certain punishment create a reliable system of justice for university students. Stoner is a lawyer, campus conflict consultant, and investigator who helps colleges address judicial affairs issues. Steinbach is a lawyer and education consultant who focuses on legal issues faced by higher education institutions.

The student-disciplinary codes of colleges have received rough treatment in the news media recently [April 1997]. Many stories have been questioning or second-guessing the efforts of officials to deal with student misconduct.

Student-affairs officials began the 1996 academic year as they always do, informing students about how they are expected to behave and training residence-hall advisers and members of disciplinary boards about ways to ensure safe living and learning environments for students.

But it is clear that all of us who are involved in student discipline must work harder than we have in the past to educate the broader public—and particularly the news media—about what we are trying to accomplish. A few examples will explain why.

Colleges Hold Students to High Behavior Standards

After a male student at Virginia Polytechnic Institute and State University was accused of violence against a female student during the last academic year, the news media raised questions, often based upon incorrect assumptions and erroneous information, about how colleges deal with allegations of sexual violence between students. Two feature articles in the *New York Times* last spring displayed considerable outrage over how student-disciplinary systems operate, implying that they operate erratically or shield students from punishment for conduct that, if committed off campus, could result in jail terms for the perpetrators.

Media coverage often seems to suggest that colleges should give up their efforts to handle students' misbehavior and rely instead upon outside police and local district attorneys to handle allegations of misconduct—so that students are treated "just like" other citizens. We need to make clearer to the public why this approach cannot possibly provide the environment that students need.

Nowhere are the difficulties of explaining colleges' disciplinary practices to the public—and the likelihood of sensationalized media coverage—more apparent than in cases of sexual violence between students. Every residential college has rules against such behavior and, like many other college rules (such as those concerning stealing or the misuse of alcohol), the conduct prohibited by college rules also is barred by criminal law.

Several news stories charged that colleges tried to hush up incidents of sexual violence by substituting internal student-disciplinary proceedings for action in the civil or criminal courts. These accusations are entirely misguided because colleges' disciplinary systems are not intended to be a substitute for the courts.

They are, instead, the method by which a college enforces its own standards of behavior, which often are higher than those required by criminal law. Moreover, no college can dictate a prosecutor's decision about whether to pursue a criminal case.

Colleges Respond Immediately to Sexual Violence Allegations

Nevertheless, unfair media charges make it clear that student-affairs personnel must educate the public, as well as their campuses, about several issues regarding allegations of sexual violence.

First, such an allegation receives immediate attention from college officials. The response may include personal counseling for all students involved, as well as referral of the matter to college disciplinary officials. Students also have the option of seeking redress by pursuing a criminal complaint or a civil charge for damages; these two avenues of redress are not controlled by the college.

Incidents of sexual violence can cause enormous pain. Several factors often converge to make it difficult for honest fact-finders to determine exactly what happened: Alcohol may have been involved; there may be no witnesses other than the two students involved; and the incident sometimes has not been reported promptly. While these factors may make it difficult to

DUE PROCESS RIGHTS ASSOCIATED WITH ACADEMIC DISMISSAL AND DISCIPLINARY HEARINGS

Due Process Right	Academic Dismissal	Disciplinary Hearing
1. Timely Disposition	Mandatory but flexible	Mandatory but flexible (*Cobb v. Rector and Visitors of the University of Virginia*)
2. Notice	Mandatory	Mandatory (*Dixon v. Alabama Board of Education*)
3. Adherence to established procedures	Recommended	Recommended (*Goodreau v. Rector and Visitors of the University of Virginia* and *Jones v. The Board of Governors of the University of North Carolina et al.*)
4. Hearing	Formal hearing not required (*Board of Curators of the University of Missouri et al. v. Horowitz*)	Hearing is mandatory (*Dixon v. Alabama State Board of Education*) Hearing not required for appeals (*Goodreau v. Rector and Visitors of the University of Virginia*) Accused has the right to be present (*Tigrett v. Rector and Visitors of the University of Virginia*)
5. Assistance of Student Advocate	Not required	Advisable but not required (*Cobb v. Rector and Visitors of the University of Virginia* and *Jaska v. Regents of the University of Michigan*)
6. Right to Presence of Counsel	Not required	Unless criminal charges are pending, there is no right to have an attorney present. (*Gabrilowitz. v. Newman*)
7. Substantive Due Process	Required	Required (*Dixon v. Alabama State Board of Education*)

Taken from: Claire R. La Roche, "Student Rights Associated with Disciplinary and Academic Hearings and Sanctions," *College Student Journal*, vol. 39, no. 1, March 2005.

treat each student fairly, colleges and universities cannot shirk their responsibility to try.

Colleges Offer Victims Informed Options for Justice

The public, as well as everyone on campus, must be helped to understand that leaving conduct that may violate both criminal law and college standards solely in the hands of the local police would guarantee a horrible result: The environment on campus would be no different from that on the streets.

Moreover, after administrators have spent years trying to assure students that complaints about serious matters such as sexual violence will be dealt with promptly and fairly, it is simply not appropriate to consider doing nothing except calling the police and waiting for them to act.

Furthermore, the public and the media should realize that the counseling that campus officials provide to victims cannot really be considered adequate unless officials explain that prosecutors will rarely undertake an alleged "date rape" case unless the victim can show evidence of physical abuse, such as bruises, or can produce witnesses who can corroborate critical facts. This reflects the reality that prosecutors must have enough evidence in criminal cases to prove guilt "beyond a reasonable doubt."

Campus officials also must discuss with the alleged victim the heavy toll that a criminal case may take on the accuser. Unfortunately, our criminal-law system still often exposes a rape victim to a protracted, painful, and public ordeal.

To say, as some media reports have, that a frank discussion of this problem unreasonably "discourages" victims from pressing criminal charges, or reflects an attempt to "hush up" an incident, is to ignore the best interests of the victim and to misunderstand the nature of counseling. The victim needs to be told of the alternatives available, and to weigh their respective costs and benefits, to make an informed decision about what to do.

Moreover, if students believe that campus officials will force victims of sexual violence to report the incidents to law-enforcement authorities, many will be unwilling to report sexual assaults to anyone. This would have serious, adverse consequences for both alleged victims and the campus as a whole.

College Discipline Promotes a Positive Learning Environment

Some critics have charged that colleges and universities prefer to use their own disciplinary procedures so that offenders will receive only trivial punishments, even though they may deserve far harsher treatment under criminal law. Regrettably, there may have been cases in which a college or university pursued a self-serving course, minimizing adverse publicity at the expense of fairness for students.

In the vast majority of cases, however, colleges are doing precisely what they should be doing. They are apprising the alleged victim of available alternatives and resources and approaching each case based on its particular facts, with an eye to the best interests of all of the students involved.

When the evidence warrants, campus disciplinary proceedings ordinarily should be initiated and brought to a reasonably prompt conclusion whether or not criminal proceedings are under way. But colleges are not law-enforcement institutions; their mission is education. After all, the harshest punishment they can hand out is expulsion from college, not a jail term.

When they conduct disciplinary proceedings, they are not trying to imitate courts, with their threats of imprisonment or possible awards of monetary damages. Instead, they are trying to promote an environment conducive to learning by showing those who misbehave—and students generally—exactly what kind of behavior is expected of them.

Thus, a college has a strong interest in disciplining those who disrupt the campus community, whether or not the same conduct has been or could be punished under criminal law.

Students embrace on the main campus of Virginia Polytechnic Institute and State University (Virginia Tech), a school whose disciplinary system came under scrutiny from the media. © Mario Tama/Staff/Getty Images.

The College System Can Offer Confidentiality

Some critics complain that colleges and universities lack defined or enforceable disciplinary procedures, but campus proceedings do not have to follow the same rigid procedures that are used in criminal law. Most colleges, however, have gone to great lengths in recent years to spell out their disciplinary processes and to see that they are followed routinely.

When both the accuser and the accused are students, colleges generally try to provide each party with fair and conscientious counseling and, if the facts warrant, a formal hearing. The student who is accused of violating college rules is entitled to know the charges and generally to have an opportunity to be heard.

But the courts never have held that colleges must afford accused students the same rights that apply under criminal law: to be represented by an attorney or to conduct the kind of cross-examination that plays such a prominent (and dramatic) role in criminal prosecutions.

And in most states, college disciplinary proceedings may be conducted with less publicity—sometimes confidentially—while all states require criminal trials to be public. Disciplinary proceedings try to emphasize the educational nature of the student-discipline process.

College proceedings often provide a better means of resolving accusations of sexual violence than do criminal procedures. Some student victims, knowing that the public trials often vilify victims of sexual violence, are relieved to be given the choice of having their complaints heard in a confidential disciplinary proceeding that respects the dignity of everyone involved.

College Systems Succeed When the Criminal System Has Failed

Thus, critics are misguided when they charge that college disciplinary systems provide students with "sanctuary" from the criminal law. The opposite is true. Students who misbehave are subject not only to the criminal- and civil-justice systems but also to the possibility of being disciplined or expelled from college.

Illustrating this point is a case at St. John's University, in New York, a few years ago, in which students acquitted in criminal court of rape charges nonetheless were found in violation of the college's rules and were expelled.

Rather than retreat from the challenge of dealing with student misbehavior, as some critics urge, colleges must continue to work hard to communicate to the public the complex, but vital, message about the role that student disciplinary procedures play in academe. If they do not, we may face further misguided attacks on our efforts to enforce student-conduct rules.

> *"[Colleges] should avoid using one-size-fits-all standardized discipline codes and instead develop codes that respond specifically to each of their institutions' particular situations . . ."*

College Disciplinary Codes and Approaches Should Not Be Legalistic

Peter F. Lake

In the following viewpoint, Peter F. Lake, the director of the Center for Excellence in Higher Education Law and Policy at the Stetson University College of Law, criticizes the adoption of legalistic codes of discipline by institutions of higher education. He argues that the use of legalistic language and proceedings is inconsistent with US Supreme Court rulings on higher education discipline and creates an overly complicated system that confuses students and fails to provide meaningful guidelines for behavior. Lake suggests that colleges implement more individualized systems, which he terms master academic plans, to offer students mentor-based relationships that will help them to navigate the entire course of their college career. Lake is the author of the book Beyond Discipline: Managing the Modern Higher Education Environment.

In their efforts to manage the college environment, many higher-education institutions have deployed complex systems of student discipline—often in the form of legalistic codes of conduct. But, paradoxically, the major challenges involving students on our campuses appear to be getting worse: High-risk alcohol and drug use persists at dangerous levels. Student mental-health issues have never been more prominent. Cheating and a lack of respect for academic integrity are epidemic. The list goes on.

Administrators have commonly believed that student disciplinary codes are legally required or will help combat the risk of litigation. But the US Supreme Court has never required colleges to have such legalistic codes and procedures, and those systems now seem to struggle to meet the challenges of the modern university. In fact, the very idea of discipline seems misplaced in higher education today.

Before the 1960s, the law had almost no role in regulating higher education. The earliest American colleges were typically viewed as charitable corporations, and power was usually divided between those who administered the institution under its governing rules and those who ensured that donors' intent was being faithfully followed. Over the years donor influence declined, and control of the academic environment became concentrated in the hands of each institution's governing body and administrators. At that time, the law provided no redress for what today would be viewed as obvious wrongs committed by administrators and faculty members on students.

The Supreme Court Never Fully Mandated Due Process

The first case to seriously challenge the power and prerogative of a college to manage students in whatever ways it saw fit was *Dixon v. Alabama* (1961), which is often heralded as the fountainhead of due process in American higher-education law. In that case, a federal appellate court ruled that six black students

According to some education experts, Millennial students respond better to mentors, role models, personal relationships, and individualized attention than to strict codes of conduct. © Erik Dreyer/Getty Images.

who had participated in civil-rights protests and been expelled without a hearing had the right to defend themselves. But the Supreme Court never fully adopted *Dixon*'s sweeping application of due-process principles to college students.

Indeed, the Supreme Court ducked issues of due process for college students for almost two decades. Then, in *Board of Curators of the University of Missouri v. Horowitz* (1978) and *Regents of the University of Michigan v. Ewing* (1985)—both cases that presented the issue of whether colleges could dismiss students in medical programs without due process—the court declined to hold squarely that higher education owed students due-process rights. In *Ewing*, for example, the court ruled that "considerations of profound importance counsel restrained judicial review of the substance of academic decisions."

Since then, the only cases in which the Supreme Court has significantly interfered with colleges' prerogatives to manage students on their own campuses have involved First Amendment or discrimination issues. In essence, the court has held that institutions should have some procedures in place to protect against a manifest factual error being committed that could seriously injure a student. But when decisions involve the exercise of judgment and weighing, and do not admit of simple true-or-false fact verification, such matters are best left to the kinds of academic processes that academics typically pursue. Indeed, the court has viewed overly legalistic systems as inconsistent with educational objectives.

Colleges Adopted Legalistic Discipline Models

Yet despite that message from the Supreme Court, colleges have overwhelmingly chosen legalistic discipline models, probably because the law entered the American higher-education consciousness for the first time in the 1960s, right when law as a tool for social reform was at an all-time zenith. Colleges also understandably turned to lawyers to assist in ensuring legal compliance after *Dixon*, and, once involved, lawyers had a tendency to offer legalistic solutions to all types of problems and issues.

Most recently, two trends have emerged in litigation regarding student disciplinary processes. First, some courts now seem to take the position that if higher education wishes to provide legalistic due process, then it will be required to truly provide it. In other words, if colleges are administering mini-court systems, they will be held to the legal standards applicable to court systems.

Second, some courts, beginning with the *Schaer v. Brandeis* (2000) case in Massachusetts, have taken a rather dim view of legalisms. In the Schaer case, a male student was charged with sexual misconduct and challenged the complex system that

Brandeis had in place to protect student rights. Claiming multiple errors in the system, he took his complaint all the way to the Massachusetts Supreme Judicial Court. The Massachusetts Supreme Judicial Court, in a closely divided opinion, held that Brandeis provided substantial fairness. But in sweeping language, it questioned the wisdom of attempting to deploy such legalistic approaches and courtlike processes in higher-education institutions.

Legalistic Discipline Does Not Suit Millennial Students

In addition to evolving legal trends, college populations have changed in the past decade. Millennial students—those who were born in 1982 or later and started coming to campuses in the early 2000s—have several generational traits, according to many research studies, that do not dispose them to management by legalistic discipline systems. . . .

To protect their self-esteem, Millennials have grown up constantly rewarded, not punished. Highly complex rule systems with harsh consequences are foreign to people who have been praised for even the smallest successes and whose mistakes have often been glossed over as part of a process of becoming "a better me."

Millennials typically have trouble understanding rules as guides for their behavior, unless particularized to them. They have difficulty turning abstract, objective criteria into action steps for themselves without guidance. Discipline officers frequently mention that a student will violate a rule and when confronted with that violation, respond, "I didn't understand this applied to me." When confronted with rules, whether fully understanding them or not, Millennials instinctively respond with avoidance behaviors. If they don't like what a college requires or provides, they simply find a way around it. For example, if students are dissatisfied with an institution's "safe transportation" system, or with the lack thereof, they will use their own cars and cellphones to create a livery service.

Restorative Justice Promotes Inclusion over Sanctioning

In a review of college judicial affairs practices, [students affairs professor John Wesley] Lowery and [Michael] Dannells argue that college student discipline has become too much like the criminal justice system. "The primary weakness resulting from these overly legalistic student judicial affairs systems is the creation of an increasingly adversarial environment. Within this environment, the educational focus of student judicial affairs is often lost." This is true of the proceedings as well as a relatively standardized continuum of sanctions. Students are given warnings, their privileges are restricted (such as preventing them from participating in intercollegiate sports or in other co-curricular clubs), they are removed from campus housing, suspended, or ultimately expelled. Thus, a student already operating at the margins of social acceptability is progressively outcast from membership in the conventional college community. The restorative justice approach promotes inclusion over social distancing, emphasizing instead sanctioning strategies that rebuild conventional social ties to the college community.

David Karp and Susanne Conrad,
"Restorative Justice and College Student Misconduct," Public Organization Review, *vol. 5,*
no. 4, December 2005.

Today colleges' disciplinary codes and procedures are premised on a vision of individual adult students making free decisions. But singling people out for discipline confuses Millennials, who often make their decisions in close connection with family members and friends.

Millennials are highly motivated to change behavior when rewards are at stake. Even modest rewards, such as minimal praise in a classroom setting, can spur students to change.

Colleges now feature systems of student self-governance, including honor codes, that Baby Boomers might have loved when they were in school but that Millennials would not choose for themselves, based on the traits that I've described. Indeed, they routinely say that they most want mentors, role models, and relationships.

Legalism Should Be Limited in School Codes of Conduct

As a result of such trends, colleges should move to reduce the quantity and pervasiveness of legalisms when it comes to dealing with student issues. They should avoid using one-size-fits-all standardized discipline codes and instead develop codes that respond specifically to each of their institutions' particular situations. Every effort should be made to develop processes that are educationally sound, not legalistic.

Thus, for example, colleges should look to trim complex procedural requirements to allow swifter decision making. They should consider abandoning strict standards of evidence such as "beyond a reasonable doubt" or "preponderance of the evidence," and talk more in terms of the kind of information that educators would want and need to make decisions. Also, institutions should stop placing so much emphasis on sanctions and move to create more systems of rewards.

While institutions will undoubtedly still have a number of rules, every rule statement in a code or policy should include an explanation of the spirit of that rule—the principles, values, standards that the rule hopes to enforce or foster. As part of that, colleges must accept the fact that certain of those standards, principles, and values will not necessarily translate directly into any one rule or set of rules. A prime example arises from the persistent issues involving hate speech on public campuses. The First Amendment prohibits public institutions from censoring speech through rules that punish unwanted speech. But nothing prohibits an institution from articulating its values. And, most often, the best way to combat hate speech is with education about core values, not with rules.

The Causes of Discipline Problems Must Be Addressed

College must also go [to] the heart of the issue: why they have discipline problems in the first place. At its most fundamental level, disciplinary activity is often caused by the failure of academe to anticipate issues and challenges students will face. Students often drift into, and through, our institutions. Sadly, many enter college with poorly formed ideas about the value of a college education and the real reasons that motivated them to attend. Moreover, students often have widely incoherent individual aspirations that no academic environment can satisfy. Lack of adequate preparation, focus, and intentionality leads to discipline problems. Without some program of support, those students are doomed to fail.

Thus, at the very least, students should develop master academic plans—or MAP's—for themselves, guided and aided by administrators and college personnel. Before a student arrives at an institution to claim residential space or enter classes, he or she should have engaged in a comprehensive planning process, one that continues throughout that student's academic career. The master academic plan should be viewed as an organic document that will change over time.

As part of the process, students would be assigned long-term mentors whose positions supersede and incorporate a great deal of current campus advising systems, which typically do not counsel students in a comprehensive, individualized, and continuing way. A new MAP system like the one I envision could, for instance, assign each student a primary mentor who then serves to arrange other services—retention programs, mental-health clinics, career advising—throughout a student's entire time at the institution. That is just one example; such a system could be organized in any number of ways.

Individualized Mentoring Would Benefit Students

Mentors and students would attempt to identify realistic and achievable goals and desirable outcomes, and do so in the context of understanding the opportunities and challenges that lie ahead. Part of the plan might be as simple as determining that a student should not go home to visit family and friends more than two weekends in a semester. Or, some students who have histories of alcohol or drug use might wish to establish specific rules for their own behavior.

At first glance, the idea of master academic plans may seem to be an expensive proposition for institutions, especially those with thousands of students. But many self-assessment tools, such as those that help determine personality traits or learning profiles and that require little or no expense or administrative time for students to gain large benefits, could be used. Costs could also be reduced by redirecting staff members from other similar functions, like academic advising.

At the same time, colleges could use the master academic plan to establish positive and negative consequences related to how the student interacts with others on the campus and the institution in general. That is the realm in which student codes now dwell, but the MAP process would allow institutions to individualize their expectations. For instance, if a student complies with her master plan and does not regularly go home on weekends but instead positively engages in campus life, she may receive not only praise from her mentor but also other benefits, such as "merits" that could accumulate and be used to receive preference in a housing lottery, for example. A MAP process could also help identify seriously risky and at-risk students—before it becomes too late.

Students Must Help Themselves

Certainly, colleges will seek to have comprehensive systems that govern all students equally at all times. But colleges overemphasize those systems as a way to manage their environment. The mistake most institutions make is to assume that because objective and broad standards are necessary components of a well-ordered campus community, they are sufficient on their own to create that community. The master academic plan would be individualized and structured to achieve what's also required: a higher level of intentionality, and a cause and consequence for each student.

The focus of higher education has shifted from preserving the power and prerogative of donors and institutions to empowering students. The emphasis on students requires a movement away from legalisms, codes, and discipline toward helping students help themselves. Such an approach will provide the type of service students both desire and need to succeed and thrive in higher education today.

> "The State is constrained to recognize
> a student's legitimate entitlement
> to a public education as a property
> interest which is protected by the
> Due Process Clause."

Students Must Be Granted a Hearing Before Being Suspended or Expelled by a School in Accordance with the Fourteenth Amendment

The US Supreme Court's Decision

Byron White

After participating in actions that damaged school property and interrupted the school day, nine students at Marion-Franklin High School in Columbus, Ohio, were punished with ten-day suspensions. Because none of the students were given any formal notice of the suspension or told why their actions warranted such punishment, these students appealed to the Ohio court system, alleging that their due process rights had been violated. After lower state courts ruled in favor of the students, the school board appealed the ruling all the way to the US Supreme Court. In its

Byron White, Opinion of the Court, *Goss v. Lopez*, US Supreme Court, January 22, 1975.

ruling, US Supreme Court Justice Byron White gave the court's opinion, which again ruled in favor of the students. In the following viewpoint, White maintains that all students in the United States are guaranteed the right to a public education and cannot be denied this right without the observance of due process. He rules that students must be given notice of their offense and granted the opportunity to respond to any charges in a hearing. However, his ruling stops short of prescribing a federal mandate, leaving schools the option to suspend students without a hearing in extenuating circumstances.

At the outset, appellants contend that, because there is no constitutional right to an education at public expense, the Due Process Clause does not protect against expulsions from the public school system. This position misconceives the nature of the issue, and is refuted by prior decisions. The Fourteenth Amendment forbids the State to deprive any person of life, liberty, or property without due process of law. Protected interests in property are normally "not created by the Constitution. Rather, they are created and their dimensions are defined" by an independent source such as state statutes or rules entitling the citizen to certain benefits. *Board of Regents v. Roth*, (1972). . . .

Students Have the Right to a Public Education

Here, on the basis of state law, appellees plainly had legitimate claims of entitlement to a public education. Ohio Rev. Code Ann. §§ 3313.48 and 3313.64 (1972 and Supp. 1973) direct local authorities to provide a free education to all residents between five and 21 years of age, and a compulsory attendance law requires attendance for a school year of not less than 32 weeks. It is true that § 3313.66 of the Code permits school principals to suspend students for up to 10 days; but suspensions may not be imposed without any grounds whatsoever. All of the schools had their own rules specifying the grounds for expulsion or suspension.

Having chosen to extend the right to an education to people of appellees' class generally, Ohio may not withdraw that right on grounds of misconduct, absent fundamentally fair procedures to determine whether the misconduct has occurred.

Although Ohio may not be constitutionally obligated to establish and maintain a public school system, it has nevertheless done so, and has required its children to attend. Those young people do not "shed their constitutional rights" at the schoolhouse door. *Tinker v. Des Moines School Dist.* (1969).

> "The Fourteenth Amendment, as now applied to the States, protects the citizen against the State itself and all of its creatures—Boards of Education not excepted." *West Virginia Board of Education v. Barnette* (1943).

The authority possessed by the State to prescribe and enforce standards of conduct in its schools although concededly very broad, must be exercised consistently with constitutional safeguards. Among other things, the State is constrained to recognize a student's legitimate entitlement to a public education as a property interest which is protected by the Due Process Clause and which may not be taken away for misconduct without adherence to the minimum procedures required by that Clause.

The Due Process Clause also forbids arbitrary deprivations of liberty. "Where a person's good name, reputation, honor, or integrity is at stake because of what the government is doing to him," the minimal requirements of the Clause must be satisfied. *Wisconsin v. Constantineau* (1971); *Board of Regents v. Roth*. School authorities here suspended appellees from school for periods of up to 10 days based on charges of misconduct. If sustained and recorded, those charges could seriously damage the students' standing with their fellow pupils and their teachers as well as interfere with later opportunities for higher education and employment. It is apparent that the claimed right of the State to determine unilaterally and without process whether that misconduct has occurred immediately collides with the requirements of the Constitution.

US Supreme Court Justice Byron White wrote the court decision that ruled in favor of Ohio high school students who were punished without due process. © David Hume Kennerly/Getty Images.

Suspension Constitutes a Serious Event

Appellants proceed to argue that, even if there is a right to a public education protected by the Due Process Clause generally, the Clause comes into play only when the State subjects a student to a "severe detriment or grievous loss." The loss of 10 days, it is said, is neither severe nor grievous and the Due Process Clause is therefore of no relevance. Appellants' argument is again refuted by our prior decisions; for in determining

> "whether due process requirements apply in the first place, we must look not to the "weight" but to the *nature* of the interest at stake." *Board of Regents v. Roth.*

Appellees were excluded from school only temporarily, it is true, but the length and consequent severity of a deprivation, while another factor to weigh in determining the appropriate form of hearing, "is not decisive of the basic right" to a hearing of some kind. *Fuentes v. Shevin* (1972). The Court's view has been that, as long as a property deprivation is not *de minimis* [minimal], its gravity is irrelevant to the question whether account must be taken of the Due Process Clause. A 10-day suspension from school is not *de minimis*, in our view, and may not be imposed in complete disregard of the Due Process Clause.

A short suspension is, of course, a far milder deprivation than expulsion. But, "education is perhaps the most important function of state and local governments," *Brown v. Board of Education* (1954), and the total exclusion from the educational process for more than a trivial period, and certainly if the suspension is for 10 days, is a serious event in the life of the suspended child. Neither the property interest in educational benefits temporarily denied nor the liberty interest in reputation, which is also implicated, is so insubstantial that suspensions may constitutionally be imposed by any procedure the school chooses, no matter how arbitrary.

Notice of Charges Must Be Given

"Once it is determined that due process applies, the question remains what process is due." *Morrissey v. Brewer* [1972]. We turn to that question, fully realizing, as our cases regularly do, that the interpretation and application of the Due Process Clause are intensely practical matters, and that "[t]he very nature of due process negates any concept of inflexible procedures universally applicable to every imaginable situation." *Cafeteria Workers v. McElroy* (1961). We are also mindful of our own admonition:

> "Judicial interposition in the operation of the public school system of the Nation raises problems requiring care and restraint. . . . By and large, public education in our Nation is committed to the control of state and local authorities." *Epperson v. Arkansas* (1968).

There are certain benchmarks to guide us, however. *Mullane v. Central Hanover Trust Co.* (1950), a case—often invoked by later opinions, said that

> [m]any controversies have raged about the cryptic and abstract words of the Due Process Clause but there can be no doubt that, at a minimum they require that deprivation of life, liberty or property by adjudication be preceded by notice and opportunity for hearing appropriate to the nature of the case.

"The fundamental requisite of due process of law is the opportunity to be heard," *Grannis v. Ordean* (1914), a right that "has little reality or worth unless one is informed that the matter is pending and can choose for himself whether to . . . contest." *Mullane v. Central Hanover Trust Co.* At the very minimum, therefore, students facing suspension and the consequent interference with a protected property interest must be given some kind of notice and afforded some kind of hearing. "Parties whose rights are to be affected are entitled to be heard; and in order that they may enjoy that right they must first be notified." *Baldwin v. Hale* (1864).

BIG-CITY SUSPENSIONS BY DISTRICT, 2008	
District	Suspensions Per 100 Students
Chicago, IL	13
Houston, TX	11
Dallas, TX	10
Los Angeles, CA	9
Palm Beach, FL	8
Miami-Dade County, FL	5
Fairfax County, VA	4
Broward County, FL	4
New York, NY	*1

* Note: New York City youth advocates question the number of suspensions in their city but concede that temporary-detention schools have lowered the number of suspensions as they have been used as an alternative method of punishment. No data was received from Washington, DC, Detroit, or Philadelphia even after repeated calls for it.

Taken from: *Catalyst Chicago* analysis of Illinois State Board of Education data and local school districts. Charter school data is not included.

Notice Helps Ensure Fairness

It also appears from our cases that the timing and content of the notice and the nature of the hearing will depend on appropriate accommodation of the competing interests involved. The student's interest is to avoid unfair or mistaken exclusion from the educational process, with all of its unfortunate consequences. The Due Process Clause will not shield him from suspensions properly imposed, but it disserves both his interest and the interest of the State if his suspension is, in fact, unwarranted. The concern would be mostly academic if the disciplinary process were a totally accurate, unerring process, never mistaken and never unfair. Unfortunately, that is not the case, and no one suggests that it is. Disciplinarians, although proceeding in utmost good faith, frequently act on the reports and advice of others; and the controlling facts and the nature of the conduct under challenge are often disputed. The risk of error is not at all trivial, and it should be guarded against if that may be done without prohibitive cost or interference with the educational process.

The difficulty is that our schools are vast and complex. Some modicum of discipline and order is essential if the educational function is to be performed. Events calling for discipline are frequent occurrences, and sometimes require immediate, effective action. Suspension is considered not only to be a necessary tool to maintain order, but a valuable educational device. The prospect of imposing elaborate hearing requirements in every suspension case is viewed with great concern, and many school authorities may well prefer the untrammeled power to act unilaterally, unhampered by rules about notice and hearing. But it would be a strange disciplinary system in an educational institution if no communication was sought by the disciplinarian with the student in an effort to inform him of his dereliction and to let him tell his side of the story in order to make sure that an injustice is not done. "[F]airness can rarely be obtained by secret, one-sided determination of facts decisive of rights. . . ."

> "Secrecy is not congenial to truth-seeking, and self-righteousness gives too slender an assurance of rightness. No better instrument has been devised for arriving at truth than to give a person in jeopardy of serious loss notice of the case against him and opportunity to meet it." *Anti-Fascist Committee v. McGrath* [1951].

We do not believe that school authorities must be totally free from notice and hearing requirements if their schools are to operate with acceptable efficiency. Students facing temporary suspension have interests qualifying for protection of the Due Process Clause, and due process requires, in connection with a suspension of 10 days or less, that the student be given oral or written notice of the charges against him and, if he denies them, an explanation of the evidence the authorities have and an opportunity to present his side of the story. The Clause requires at least these rudimentary precautions against unfair or mistaken findings of misconduct and arbitrary exclusion from school.

Exceptions to Due Process Do Exist

In holding as we do, we do not believe that we have imposed procedures on school disciplinarians which are inappropriate in a classroom setting. Instead we have imposed requirements which are, if anything, less than a fair-minded school principal would impose upon himself in order to avoid unfair suspensions. Indeed, according to the testimony of the principal of Marion-Franklin High School, that school had an informal procedure, remarkably similar to that which we now require, applicable to suspensions generally but which was not followed in this case. Similarly, according to the most recent memorandum applicable to the entire CPSS [Columbus Public School System], school principals in the CPSS are now required by local rule to provide at least as much as the constitutional minimum which we have described.

Hearings Do Not Have to Resemble Court Proceedings

We stop short of construing the Due Process Clause to require, countrywide, that hearings in connection with short suspensions must afford the student the opportunity to secure counsel, to confront and cross-examine witnesses supporting the charge, or to call his own witnesses to verify his version of the incident.

Brief disciplinary suspensions are almost countless. To impose in each such case even truncated trial-type procedures might well overwhelm administrative facilities in many places and, by diverting resources, cost more than it would save in educational effectiveness. Moreover, further formalizing the suspension process and escalating its formality and adversary nature may not only make it too costly as a regular disciplinary tool, but also destroy its effectiveness as part of the teaching process.

On the other hand, requiring effective notice and informal hearing permitting the student to give his version of the events will provide a meaningful hedge against erroneous action. At least the disciplinarian will be alerted to the existence of disputes about facts and arguments about cause and effect. He may then determine himself to summon the accuser, permit cross-examination, and allow the student to present his own witnesses. In more difficult cases, he may permit counsel. In any event, his discretion will be more informed and we think the risk of error substantially reduced.

"The consequences of relying on
removing children from school as a
primary tactic to address misbehavior
are nothing short of devastating."

School Expulsion: A Life Sentence?

Sarah Biehl

In the viewpoint that follows, Sarah Biehl, a staff attorney for the Ohio Poverty Law Center, argues that schools' overzealous use of suspension and expulsion as methods of punishment threatens students as well as their families and communities. The consequences cited by the author for students who are removed from school include higher dropout rates, difficulty finding a job, underemployment, and increased sexual activity at a young age. Biehl maintains that these spread to the individual's family and community, creating a cycle of poverty and destruction. These far-reaching impacts, according to the author, can be traced to the relative ease with which a school can suspend or expel a child, a situation that Biehl urges lawyers to take an active role in combating. Action is necessary, in Biehl's view, to help a generation of children become productive, contributing members of society.

Expelling a child from school and sentencing a child to life in prison without possibility of parole are two very different actions. They have different motivations and are vastly different deprivations of a child's rights. They are, however, both serious actions that carry with them consequential and long-lasting effects on a child's potential for "the full and harmonious development of his or her personality," as well as a child's rights to development, education, and an adequate standard of living as set out in the *Convention on the Rights of the Child*. Preamble, Art. 6, 27, 29, Nov. 20, 1989. Both actions also signify a profound statement about the United States' view of its obligation to ensure that children "should be fully prepared to live an individual life in society, and brought up in the spirit of the ideals proclaimed in the Charter of the United Nations, and in particular the spirit of peace, dignity, tolerance, freedom, equality and solidarity." *Id.*, Preamble.

The U.S. Supreme Court's decision last year in *Graham v. Florida*, which prohibited life sentences without possibility of parole for juveniles in non-homicide cases, confirmed that, at least for life sentences, children's rights and our collective obligations to children must not be lost or overrun as part of a quest to punish wrongdoing. The *Graham* decision is notable from a children's rights perspective because, like its predecessor, *Roper v. Simmons*, 543 U.S. 551 (2005), its focus on juvenile brain development as a justification for precluding life sentences shifts jurisprudential focus away from the horrendousness of the crime committed and toward the development and future potential of the child involved. See *Graham v. Florida*, 130 S. Ct. 2011, 2026–27 (2010). As the Court explained in *Graham*, the determination of whether a punishment is cruel and unusual by Eighth Amendment standards "requires consideration of the culpability of the offenders at issue in light of their crimes and characteristics, along with the severity of the punishment in question." *Id.* at 2026 (citing *Roper*, 543 U.S. at 568). The Court went on to explain that children are different from adults and should be treated differently because "parts of the brain involved in behavior control continue to mature through late adolescence." *Id.* Thus, "[j]uveniles are more capable of change than are adults, and their actions are less likely to be evidence of 'irretrievably depraved characteristics.'" Id. (quoting *Roper*, 543 U.S. at 570).

The *Graham* holding and the social science-based data that motivated it create an interesting context from which to analyze the school discipline crisis that grips the United States. If life sentences without the possibility of parole for juveniles in non-homicide cases are clearly unconstitutional, and if what we now know and understand about the way children's brains develop justifies holding children not accountable in the same way as adults, then how can our legal and educational systems continue to justify the relative ease with which school administrators expel children from school? The stakes and the legal analyses are different, but the consequences to children and to the nation as a whole are perhaps no less serious.

Since the 1970s, school suspension and expulsion rates in the United States have more than doubled to more than three million suspensions and over 97,000 expulsions in the year 2000. NAACP Legal Defense and Education Fund, *Dismantling the School to Prison Pipeline* (October 2005). "Zero-tolerance" discipline policies have fueled the increase in recent years, as has the increasing reliance of school administrators and educators on law enforcement tactics to discipline children. See Advancement Project, *Education on Lockdown: The Schoolhouse to Jailhouse Track* (March 2005); American Civil Liberties Union, *Dignity Denied: The Effect of "Zero Tolerance" Policies on Students' Human Rights* (Nov. 2008)

Recently, the news media has exposed the often outrageous consequences of zero tolerance and the heightened role of law enforcement in school that flows from these policies. This exposure highlights the policies' absurd results. Examples include a six-year-old Cub Scout in Delaware who was suspended from school for bringing a camping utensil with a knife, fork, and spoon on it

Debbie Christie attends a school board meeting in 2009. Her son Zachary, a Cub Scout, was suspended for bringing a camping utensil to school. © AP Photo/Steve Ruark.

to school and a 12-year-old girl in Brooklyn, New York, who was arrested and hauled out of school in handcuffs for doodling on her desk. Though these stories bring fleeting attention to a misguided policy trend, they are but minor illustrations of a growing, monumental problem in our education system. Every day in the United States, hundreds and possibly even thousands of children are removed from school—for anywhere from a couple of days to a year or more—for offenses ranging from shouting in the hallway, talking back to a teacher, being "insubordinate," getting into a fight with another student, or, in more serious situations, bringing alcohol, drugs, or weapons to campus.

The consequences of relying on removing children from school as a primary tactic to address misbehavior are nothing short of devastating. Prior suspension is more likely to cause a child to drop out of high school than any other factor, including low socioeconomic status, not living with both biological parents, a high number of school changes, and having sex before age 15. Suhyun Suh, Jingyo Suh, & Irene Houston, "Predictors of Categorical At-Risk High School Dropouts," 85; *Journal of Counseling and Development, 196,* 196–203 (Spring 2007). Students who are expelled from school—that is, removed from school for more than 10 days—are even less likely to graduate from high school.

The consequences of not graduating from high school, of course, are severe. Children who do not finish high school are 3.5 times more likely to be arrested as adults. Additionally, approximately 82 percent of the adult prison population is composed of high-school dropouts. Coalition for Juvenile Justice, *Abandoned in the Back Row: New Lessons in Education and Delinquency Prevention* (2001). Children who do not finish high school are much more likely than high-school graduates to be and remain unemployed and to earn less money if they do gain employment. *Id.* Additionally, school dropouts are much more likely to receive public assistance. See National Center for Education Statistics, Dropout Rates in the United States (2000).

These trends are bad for the children and families who are directly affected by them, helping to further entrench intergenerational poverty and marginalization and effectively cutting off children's hopes for successful futures as productive adults. They are also destructive for communities as a whole because large numbers of uneducated young people who are more likely to commit crime put all of us at a greater risk of becoming victims of crime, in addition to the fact that young people who are and remain unemployed do not build strong, self-sustainable communities as adults. Bob Herbert of the *New York Times* has reported that the number of "disconnected youth"—young people between the ages of 16 and 24 who are neither in school nor working—is at least four million nationwide and growing. Bob Herbert, "Out of Sight," *N.Y. Times*, June 10, 2008. (Note that this article and the four million disconnected youth statistic were published in 2008, before the worst of the recent recession had hit families.)

Our broad, nationwide overreliance on exclusionary discipline policies is a national disaster. It is also only the tip of the iceberg. Exclusionary school discipline is only one of many factors that lead to children being "pushed out" of school. See *Dignity in Schools Campaign, National Resolution for Ending School Pushout*, December 2009. Unwelcoming school environments in many cities and communities treat students more like prisoners than children and, when combined with a lack of relevant or engaging curricula, inadequate resources and facilities, and failure to use effective prevention and intervention strategies for misbehavior, create a situation in which many children are almost destined to fail. Education, however, is not a fundamental right as set out in the Fourteenth Amendment. *San Antonio Indep. Sch. Dist. v. Rodriguez*, 411 U.S. 1, 11–12 (1973). Thus, while students are due some level of due process before their right to an education can be taken away (see *Goss v. Lopez*, 419 U.S. 565 (1975)), it is essentially quite easy for school administrators to expel them from school, dooming many of them to a life of unemployment, crime, and little else.

Each state has a different statute addressing the procedure school administrators must follow to expel a child from school. All have a starting point in *Goss v. Lopez*, which holds that removing a child from school for more than 10 days requires something more than the minimal notice and explanation that is required when suspending a child from school for less than 10 days. 419 U.S. at 581–84. The process that is required for those

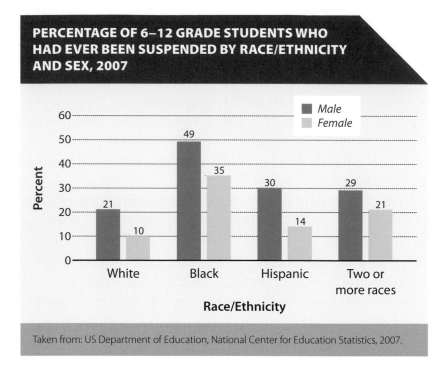

PERCENTAGE OF 6–12 GRADE STUDENTS WHO HAD EVER BEEN SUSPENDED BY RACE/ETHNICITY AND SEX, 2007

Taken from: US Department of Education, National Center for Education Statistics, 2007.

longer exclusions of more than 10 days varies from state to state, but generally involves a hearing in front of the board of education at which the student has a right to an attorney (but not at public expense) and may present his or her case, but has limited access to evidence against him or her (few states have rules against admission of hearsay, for example, and schools often rely on evidence parents and students cannot access, like video surveillance footage) and little recourse to the rules of evidence to help make his or her case. The practical result is that boards of education rarely overturn a principal's decision to expel a child from school, and, unless they have the resources or good fortune to attain an attorney, most children who have been proposed for expulsion from school are ultimately expelled.

So, given the extreme and likely consequences to children and communities that result from schools' heavy reliance on school suspension and expulsion, why is it so easy to remove children from school? The considerations the [US] Supreme Court enumerated in *Graham*—that children's brains do not fully develop the ability to control behavior until later adolescence and that they therefore cannot be held accountable for their actions in the same manner as adults who commit similar acts—seem to apply equally well to the school expulsion scenario. Children who misbehave in school are largely not criminals. They are children. They misbehave. That misbehavior, especially when it endangers others, must be addressed. But it should be addressed appropriately, with a focus on preserving every child's dignity and right to an education, because although children who get into a fight at school have done something much less onerous than children who commit the horrific crimes that motivated the *Graham* case, the reality is that the consequences for these two groups of children are both devastating.

Children who do not finish school are essentially doomed to a life sentence of crime and unemployment. Children in prison are denied any opportunity to participate in life outside prison walls. School dropouts are ostensibly free to roam the streets, but are cut off from access to the ladder to success in U.S. society and are more likely to end up in prison and in unemployment lines. Their futures are functionally as bleak as their incarcerated counterparts.

The costs to communities and the country as a whole are equally great. Draconian school discipline policies are condemning an entire generation of young people. Losing the right and/ or ability to complete their educations is a serious deprivation of children's rights. It is not equivalent to depriving a child of his or her right to liberty and right to be free from cruel and unusual punishment, but surely it is serious enough to merit more than a sham due-process procedure that ultimately puts children's futures in the hands of overzealous school administrators who have almost unfettered discretion to decide whether a child should be expelled from school. The right to education is a human right that should not be taken away from students unless states "take all appropriate measures to ensure that school discipline is administered in a manner consistent with the child's human dignity" (*Convention on the Rights of the Child*). Art. 28 (Nov 20, 1989). This is not the reality for thousands of children in the United States. This reality alone should serve as a basis for developing school discipline policies that respect children's dignity and preserve their right to an education, reserving suspension and expulsion only for the most serious, dangerous situations.

There are some concrete things that lawyers who care about children's rights can do to help. First, lawyers need to advocate, as the ABA has already suggested, for the abolishment of state, local, and school district-level zero-tolerance policies. See American Bar Association, *Resolution Concerning School Discipline* (2001). Second, lawyers can help ensure that low-income children and families facing school expulsion have legal representation by taking such cases for little or no cost and/or by supporting legal aid programs and other nonprofits that provide such representation for free. Anecdotal evidence nationally shows that legal representation in school expulsion cases greatly increases the likelihood that an individual child will avoid expulsion. Finally, and most importantly, lawyers can help support local movements to shift school district policies away from a focus on suspension and expulsion as the primary means of school discipline.

There are some great examples from all over the country of lawyers working in cooperation with community-based organizations and local parent and student-led groups to advocate for needed change. The Advancement Project, for example, is a Washington, D.C.-based civil rights organization that worked with Padres & Jóvenes Unidos, a Denver, Colorado-based parent and youth organizing group, to implement changes to the Denver Public Schools student code of conduct, reducing suspensions, expulsions, and school-based arrests. See Padres & Jóvenes Unidos, *Ending the School to Jail Track*. It is often difficult for attorneys to take a back seat, but school policies are and should be a community concern, and community-based and community-directed actions have proven to be the most effective means of achieving meaningful policy change. Children's rights lawyers, especially, can provide needed leadership, guidance, and support because they understand the stakes. The parallels between children who have been sentenced to draconian prison sentences and children who lose the right to complete their educations are stark, and the consequences of failing our children are terrifying. We can and must do better.

> "Schools should be able to establish reasonable zero tolerance policies for students who present a danger to others."

School Zero Tolerance Policies Are a Legal and Effective Means of Discipline

National School Boards Association

In September 1999, six African American students in Decatur, Illinois, were expelled for fighting at a football game. The students brought the matter to court, claiming the expulsions were racially motivated and infringed on their constitutional rights. In Fuller v. Decatur Public School Board of Education School District 61, *the district court upheld the school board's decision. The students appealed. In the following viewpoint, the National School Boards Association (NSBA) maintains that the appellate court should not alter the district court's ruling because school boards have a right to establish zero tolerance policies to keep their schools safe, and, in this case, the students knew of the policy and were informed of the charges leveled against them. The NSBA denies that these policies were applied unjustly due to the students' race because the zero tolerance statutes affect all students equally.*

Amicus brief in *Fuller v. Decatur Public School Board of Education School District 61* by the National School Boards Association, Supreme Court of the United States, May 24, 2001.

The issues raised by the appellants are not new. The Supreme Court, as well as this Circuit, has reviewed cases challenging the authority of school boards to discipline students. In *Wood v. Strickland* (1975), the Supreme Court stated clearly that "[i]t is not the role of the federal courts to set aside decisions of school administrators that the court may view as lacking a basis in wisdom or compassion. . . . "

The School Board Followed Due Process Rules

The school board involved in this case did not abuse its discretion. Moreover, the school board afforded the students adequate constitutional protections when it decided to expel the students for engaging in a violent fight in the football stands in which innocent bystanders were injured. The Illinois Compiled Statutes grant school boards broad discretion to adopt and enforce rules and regulations regarding student conduct. Section 10-22.6 allows school boards to expel or suspend students and states in pertinent part:

> To expel pupils guilty of gross disobedience or misconduct, and no action shall lie against them for such expulsion. Expulsion shall take place only after the parents have been requested to appear at a meeting of the board, or with a hearing officer appointed by it, to discuss their child's behavior. Such request shall be made by registered or certified mail and shall state the time, place and purpose of the meeting. The board, or a hearing officer appointed by it, at such meeting shall state the reasons for dismissal and the date on which the expulsion is to become effective. If a hearing officer is appointed by the board he shall report to the board a written summary of the evidence heard at the meeting and the board may take such action thereon as it finds appropriate.

In addition, that same section of the compiled statutes allows school boards to expel a student for a definite period of time not to exceed two calendar years, as determined on a case-by-case basis.

Here, each of the students and his parent or guardian was provided notice of a hearing before an independent hearing officer and before the school board. In addition, each one was apprised of the provisions of the discipline policy that they were charged with violating. The evidence showed that the parent or guardian of each of the students received this letter prior to the hearing. Finally, each of the students was presented with an opportunity to be heard and to present his version of the incident to the hearing officer and the school board. These procedures are consistent with constitutional procedural due process requirements. . . .

Many School Districts Have Adopted Zero Tolerance Policies

In their Amended Complaint, the students alleged the School Board's "no tolerance/zero tolerance policy for violence" violated their procedural and substantive due process rights. Assuming *arguendo* [for argument's sake] that the zero tolerance resolution became part of the district's official student discipline policy, that fact would not preclude a judgment in favor of the school district.

A zero tolerance policy is generally defined as a school or district policy that mandates pre-determined consequences or punishment for specific offenses, regardless of the circumstances or disciplinary history of the student involved. Schools generally consider zero tolerance policies for students who make threats of violence, engage in violent behavior, or bring weapons to school. Such a policy might include expulsion or suspension of students who threaten to kill or who seriously assault others and, when appropriate, would quickly provide for psychological evaluation or intervention for these students. A clear and consistent message that threats of violence will not be tolerated may help to reduce the actual occurrence of violence. . . .

Many states and school districts have expanded the types of offenses that will be met with a response of zero tolerance. As such, the practice of mandating a particular type of punishment has developed to include infractions beyond bringing firearms to school. As reported by the National Center for Education Statistics:

> Nine out of 10 schools reported zero tolerance policies for firearms (94%) and weapons other than firearms (91%). Eighty-seven percent of schools had zero tolerance policies for alcohol and 88% had zero tolerance policies for drugs. Most schools also had zero tolerance policies for violence (79%) and tobacco possession violations (79%). *Indicators of School Crime and Safety* (1999).

Nonetheless, it is important to note that a policy of zero tolerance does not preclude careful adherence to due process of law. Zero tolerance policies must provide for adequate procedural due process commensurate with the severity of the designated consequence. In practice, zero tolerance policies don't change the procedures provided before school officials impose discipline. Although zero tolerance policies are often described as providing "automatic" penalties, due process still must be followed. Students must still be given notice of the charges against them, a fair hearing, an opportunity to be heard, and a decision based on the merits. . . .

It is important for school districts to ensure that the designated consequences of proscribed behavior are consistent with substantive due process considerations. Policies should be carefully constructed and include clear definitions so as to not unintentionally include behavior that the school board does not wish to cover. Basically the rule and punishment must be reasonable, not arbitrary or capricious. . . .

Zero Tolerance Policies Apply Equally to All Students

Zero tolerance policies are often implemented, in part, to address the concern of discriminatory application of discipline policies. Zero tolerance policies are a way for school districts to ensure that any student, regardless of race, would receive the same

Kenneth Arndt was acting superintendent of the public schools of Decatur, Illinois, when six students were expelled for fighting at a football game in 1999. © AP Photo/Paul Beaty.

punishment for the same inappropriate behavior. In this case, the appellants have alleged that the school district has maintained a policy and practice of arbitrary and discriminatory expulsions of African-American students. However, appellants have failed to show that race played any role in the school board's expulsion decision.

The [US] Supreme Court has held that to "establish a discriminatory effect in a race case, the claimant must show that similarly situated individuals of a different race were not prosecuted." *United States v. Armstrong* (1996). . . . In *Armstrong*, the defendants, who were indicted for selling crack cocaine and using a firearm in connection with drug trafficking, alleged that they were selected for prosecution because they are black. However, the claim in *Armstrong* failed because the study upon which the defendants relied "failed to identify individuals who were not black and could have been prosecuted for the offenses for which respondents were charged, but were not so prosecuted." The decision in *Armstrong* is applicable to civil cases where plaintiffs claim discrimination on the basis of race. In a race case, "plaintiffs must show that similarly situated individuals of a different race were not subjected to the challenged conduct." Similarly, in this case the students have not identified individuals who were not black and could have been disciplined for engaging in the same or similar violent behavior that the appellants engaged in at the football game. . . .

Similarly, the students in this case have not shown that they were treated differently than any other student charged with fighting at a school function. As a matter of fact, information regarding the race of the students involved never even appeared on the hearing officers' reports, nor was the school board ever advised of the race of any student facing expulsion. As with any disciplinary policy, fair and consistent enforcement of zero tolerance policies is essential. The purpose of zero tolerance policies is to provide identical discipline for circumscribed offenses; thus there is no room for inconsistent administration of punishments. . . .

Zero Tolerance Policies Are an Effective Tool for Keeping Schools Safe

There are increasing reports that zero tolerance policies can be effective in reducing criminal and violent offenses. In Baltimore, Maryland, the school board adopted an aggressive zero tolerance policy. The policy is credited with producing a 67% decline in arrests and a 31% decline in school crime in September and October 1999, compared with the same time a year earlier. In Texas, a survey found that from 1993 to 1998, the percentage of teachers who viewed assaults on students as a "significant problem" dropped from 53% to 31%. It is during this time that Texas mandated expulsion of students for drugs and weapons on school grounds and at school events.

The decision of the district court should be upheld regardless of whether a zero tolerance policy was used to expel the students in this case. Reasonable zero tolerance policies assist school officials in maintaining safety and order in a fair, constitutionally sound manner. Reasonable zero tolerance policies specify what types of conduct will result in the automatic penalty of suspension or expulsion. For lesser violations, aggravating and mitigating circumstances should be taken into consideration. Finally, as with any discipline decision by school officials, all due process procedures must be followed and statutory and constitutional rights protected.

Schools should be able to establish reasonable zero tolerance policies for students who present a danger to others. Students who pose a threat must be dealt with under these policies and this information should be communicated to local law enforcement to assist in preventing violence in the community. The resolution adopted in this case did just that. Schools should work with their community to create partnerships with social service organizations and other service-oriented groups that can provide resources to troubled students.

Schools should not tolerate behavior that would be punished as illegal off campus. Moreover, schools should not be a haven

RATE OF RECORDED AND REPORTED CRIMES AT PUBLIC SCHOOLS PER 1,000 STUDENTS

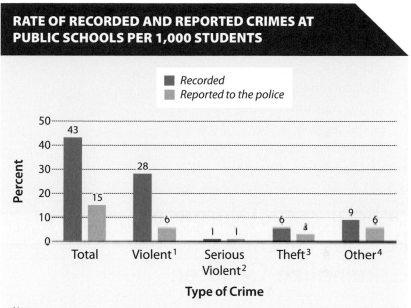

Notes:
1. Violent incidents include serious violent incidents; physical attack or fight without a weapon; and threat of physical attack without a weapon.
2. Serious violent incidents include rape or attempted rape; sexual battery other than rape; physical attack or fight with a weapon; threat of physical attack with a weapon; and robbery with or without a weapon.
3. Theft/larceny includes taking things worth over $10 without personal confrontation.
4. Other incidents include possession of a firearm or explosive device; possession of a knife or sharp object; distribution, possession, or use of illegal drugs or alcohol; and vandalism.

Taken from: US Department of Education, National Center for Education Statistics, 2007–2008 School Survey on Crime and Safety (SSOCS), 2008.

for misbehavior. Schools should be a place where students learn civic responsibility and where appropriate behavior is expected. Our nation's schools should be the safest place in America. As such, school boards and school officials need the authority to respond to student violence swiftly and appropriately. It is equally important that the courts afford them the discretion to do their job of educating responsible, law-abiding citizens.

> "We have moved into a new paradigm in America where young people are increasingly viewed as suspects and treated as criminals by school officials and law enforcement alike."

School Zero Tolerance Policies Unfairly Criminalize Children

John W. Whitehead

John W. Whitehead is an attorney and the president of the Rutherford Institute, a civil liberties defense organization. In the following viewpoint, Whitehead contends that school zero tolerance policies are too broad and constitutionally unjust. In his opinion, zero tolerance policies were initially drafted to keep guns and violence out of schools, but since then, these statutes have been expanded to cover behaviors that pose no real threat to the student body. Because of this, Whitehead fears schools are knowingly turning all students into suspects who must be monitored and controlled to keep them from committing the slightest infraction of school law.

> "We end up punishing honor students to send a message to bad kids. But the data indicate that the bad kids are not getting the message."
> —Professor Russell Skiba

Wwhat we are witnessing, thanks in large part to zero tolerance policies that were intended to make schools safer by discouraging the use of actual drugs and weapons by students, is the inhumane treatment of young people and the criminalization of childish behavior.

Criminalizing Youngsters

Ninth grader Andrew Mikel is merely the latest in a long line of victims whose educations have been senselessly derailed by school administrators lacking in both common sense and compassion. A freshman at Spotsylvania High School in Virginia, Andrew was expelled in December 2010 for shooting a handful of small pellets akin to plastic spit wads at fellow students in the school hallway during lunch period. Although the initial punishment was only for 10 days, the school board later extended it to the rest of the school year. School officials also referred the matter to local law enforcement, which initiated juvenile proceedings for criminal assault against young Andrew.

Andrew is not alone. Nine-year-old Patrick Timoney was sent to the principal's office and threatened with suspension after school officials discovered that one of his LEGOs was holding a 2-inch toy gun. That particular LEGO, a policeman, was Patrick's favorite because his father is a retired police officer. David Morales, an 8-year-old Rhode Island student, ran afoul of his school's zero tolerance policies after he wore a hat to school decorated with an American flag and tiny plastic Army figures in honor of American troops. School officials declared the hat out of bounds because the toy soldiers were carrying miniature guns. A 7-year-old New Jersey boy, described by school officials as "a nice kid" and "a good student," was reported to the police and charged with possessing an imitation firearm after he brought a toy Nerf-style gun to school. The gun shoots soft ping pong-type balls.

Things have gotten so bad that it doesn't even take a toy gun to raise the ire of school officials. A high school sophomore was suspended for violating the school's no-cell-phone policy after he took a call from his father, a master sergeant in the U.S. Army who was serving in Iraq at the time. A 12-year-old New York student was hauled out of school in handcuffs for doodling on her desk with an erasable marker. In Houston, an 8th grader was suspended for wearing rosary beads to school in memory of her grandmother (the school has a zero tolerance policy against the rosary, which the school insists can be interpreted as a sign of gang involvement). Six-year-old Cub Scout Zachary Christie was sentenced to 45 days in reform school after bringing a camping utensil to school that can serve as a fork, knife or spoon. And in Oklahoma, school officials suspended a first grader simply for using his hand to simulate a gun.

Ridiculous Consequences for Childish Behavior

What these incidents, all the result of overzealous school officials and inflexible zero tolerance policies, make clear is that we have moved into a new paradigm in America where young people are increasingly viewed as suspects and treated as criminals by school officials and law enforcement alike.

Adopted in the wake of Congress' passage of the 1994 Gun-Free Schools Act, which required a one-year expulsion for any child bringing a firearm or bomb to school, school zero tolerance policies were initially intended to address and prevent serious problems involving weapons, violence and drug and alcohol use in the schools. However, since the Columbine school shootings [in April 1999], nervous legislators and school boards have tightened their zero tolerance policies to such an extent that school officials are now empowered to punish all offenses severely, no matter how minor. Hence, an elementary school student is punished in the same way that an adult high school senior is punished. And a student who actually intends to harm others is treated the same as one who breaks the rules accidentally—or is *perceived* as breaking the rules.

Zero tolerance drug policies at schools have broadened, resulting in many students being punished for household drugs such as mouthwash, breath mints, and Alka-Seltzer. © Ted Thai/ Time & Life Pictures/Getty Images.

For instance, after students at a Texas school were assigned to write a "scary" Halloween story, one 13-year-old chose to write about shooting up a school. Although he received a passing grade on the story, school officials reported him to the police, resulting in his spending *six days in jail* before it was determined that no crime had been committed. Equally outrageous was the case in New Jersey where several kindergartners were suspended from school for three days for playing a make-believe game of "cops and robbers" during recess and *using their fingers* as guns.

With the distinctions between student offenses erased, and *all* offenses expellable, we now find ourselves in the midst of what *Time* magazine described as a "national crackdown on Alka-Seltzer." Indeed, at least 20 children in four states have been suspended from school for possession of the fizzy tablets in violation of zero tolerance drug policies. In some jurisdictions, carrying cough drops, wearing black lipstick or dying your hair blue are actually expellable offenses. Students have also been penalized for such inane "crimes" as bringing nail clippers to school, using Listerine or Scope, and carrying fold-out combs that resemble switchblades. A 13-year-old boy in Manassas, Virginia, who accepted a Certs breath mint from a classmate, was actually suspended and required to attend drug-awareness classes, while a 12-year-old boy who said he brought powdered sugar to school for a science project was charged with a felony for possessing a look-alike drug. Another 12-year-old was handcuffed and jailed after he stomped in a puddle, splashing classmates.

Why Zero Tolerance Is a Failure

The American Bar Association has rightly condemned these zero tolerance policies as being "a one-size-fits-all solution to all the problems that schools confront." Unfortunately, when challenged about the fact that under these draconian policies, a kid who shoots a spitball is punished the same as the kid who brings a gun to school, school officials often insist that their hands are tied. That rationale, however, falls apart on several counts.

First, such policies completely fail to take into account the student's intentions, nor do they take into account the long-term damage inflicted on school children. For example, as a result of the criminal charges against him, Andrew Mikel, an honor student active in Junior ROTC and in his church who had hoped to attend the U.S. Naval Academy, can no longer be considered as an applicant.

Second, these one-strike-and-you're-out policies have proven to be largely unsuccessful and been heavily criticized by such professional organizations as the National Association of School Psychologists: "[R]esearch indicates that, as implemented, zero tolerance policies are ineffective in the long run and are related to a number of negative consequences, including increased rates of school drop out and discriminatory application of school discipline practices."

Third, with the emergence of zero tolerance policies, school officials have forsaken the time-honored distinction between punishment and discipline. Namely, that schools exist to *educate* students about their rights and the law and *discipline* those who need it, while prisons exist to *punish* criminals who have been tried and found guilty of breaking the law. And, as a result, many American schools now resemble prisons with both barbed wire perimeters and police walking the halls.

Fourth, such policies *criminalize* childish, otherwise innocent behavior and in many cases create a permanent record that will haunt that child into adulthood. Moreover, by involving the police in incidents that should never leave the environs of the school, it turns the schools into little more than a police state. For example, 9-year-old Michael Parson was suspended from school for a day and ordered to undergo a psychological evaluation after mentioning to a classmate his intent to "shoot" a fellow classmate with a wad of paper. Despite the fact that the "weapon" considered suspect consisted of a wadded-up piece of moistened paper and a rubber band with which to launch it, district officials notified local police, suspended Michael under the school's zero tolerance policy, and required him to undergo a psychological evaluation before returning to class. Incredibly, local police also went to Michael's home after midnight in order to question the fourth grader about the so-called "shooting" incident.

Finally, these policies, and the school administrators who relentlessly enforce them, render young people woefully ignorant of the rights they intrinsically possess as American citizens. What's more, having failed to learn much in the way of civic education while in school, young people are being browbeaten into believing that they have no true rights and government authorities have total power and can violate constitutional rights whenever they see fit.

There's an old axiom that what children learn in school today will be the philosophy of government tomorrow. As surveillance cameras, metal detectors, police patrols, zero tolerance policies, lockdowns, drug sniffing dogs and strip searches become the norm in elementary, middle and high schools across the nation, America is on a fast track to raising up an Orwellian [after author George Orwell, one that accepts rigid government control] generation—one populated by compliant citizens accustomed to living in a police state and who march in lockstep to the dictates of the government. In other words, the schools are teaching our young people how to be obedient subjects in a totalitarian society.

> "The openness of the public school and its supervision by the community afford significant safeguards against the kinds of abuses from which the Eighth Amendment protects the prisoner."

Corporal Punishment Administered at School Does Not Constitute Cruel and Unusual Punishment

The US Supreme Court's Decision

Lewis F. Powell Jr.

On April 19, 1977, the US Supreme Court ruled in Ingraham v. Wright *that the Eighth Amendment does not prohibit schools from administering corporal punishment on students. The case was filed in Florida courts following multiple instances in which two middle school students, James Ingraham and Roosevelt Andrews, sustained relatively serious injuries after being paddled by school administrators. The petitioners maintained that the severity of the beatings qualified as cruel and unusual punishment. However, the courts did not agree with this view. In the following viewpoint, Justice Lewis F. Powell Jr. examines court precedent and finds that the Eighth Amendment should be applied only to protect criminals,*

Lewis F. Powell Jr., Majority opinion, *Ingraham v. Wright*, Supreme Court of the United States, April 19, 1977.

and students do not require this type of protection. While many states have since enacted bans on corporal punishment, this ruling left states to determine whether corporal punishment is appropriate in schools.

In addressing the scope of the Eighth Amendment's prohibition on cruel and unusual punishment, this Court has found it useful to refer to "[t]raditional common law concepts," *Powell v. Texas* (1968), and to the "attitude[s] which our society has traditionally taken." So, too, in defining the requirements of procedural due process under the Fifth and Fourteenth Amendments, the Court has been attuned to what "has always been the law of the land," *United States v. Barnett* (1964), and to "traditional ideas of fair procedure," *Greene v. McElroy* (1959). We therefore begin by examining the way in which our traditions and our laws have responded to the use of corporal punishment in public schools.

The History of Corporal Punishment in US Schools

The use of corporal punishment in this country as a means of disciplining schoolchildren dates back to the colonial period. It has survived the transformation of primary and secondary education from the colonials' reliance on optional private arrangements to our present system of compulsory education and dependence on public schools. Despite the general abandonment of corporal punishment as a means of punishing criminal offenders, the practice continues to play a role in the public education of schoolchildren in most parts of the country. Professional and public opinion is sharply divided on the practice, and has been for more than a century. Yet we can discern no trend toward its elimination.

At common law, a single principle has governed the use of corporal punishment since before the American Revolution: teachers may impose reasonable but not excessive force to discipline a child. [Eighteenth-century English jurist, judge, and politician William] Blackstone catalogued among the "absolute rights of individuals" the right "to security from the corporal insults of menaces, assaults, beating, and wounding," but he did not regard it a "corporal insult" for a teacher to inflict "moderate correction" on a child in his care. To the extent that force was "necessary to answer the purposes for which [the teacher] is employed," Blackstone viewed it as "justifiable or lawful." The basic doctrine has not changed. . . . To the extent that the force is excessive or unreasonable, the educator in virtually all States is subject to possible civil and criminal liability.

Although the early cases viewed the authority of the teacher as deriving from the parents, the concept of parental delegation has been replaced by the view—more consonant with compulsory education laws—that the State itself may impose such corporal punishment as is reasonably necessary "for the proper education of the child and for the maintenance of group discipline." F. Harper & F. James, *Law of Torts* (1956). All of the circumstances are to be taken into account in determining whether the punishment is reasonable in a particular case. Among the most important considerations are the seriousness of the offense, the attitude and past behavior of the child, the nature and severity of the punishment, the age and strength of the child, and the availability of less severe but equally effective means of discipline. . . .

Against this background of historical and contemporary approval of reasonable corporal punishment, we turn to the constitutional question before us.

The Eighth Amendment Applies to Criminals

The Eighth Amendment provides: "Excessive bail shall not be required, nor excessive fines imposed, nor cruel and unusual punishments inflicted." Bail, fines, and punishment traditionally have been associated with the criminal process, and, by subjecting the three to parallel limitations, the text of the Amendment suggests an intention to limit the power of those entrusted with

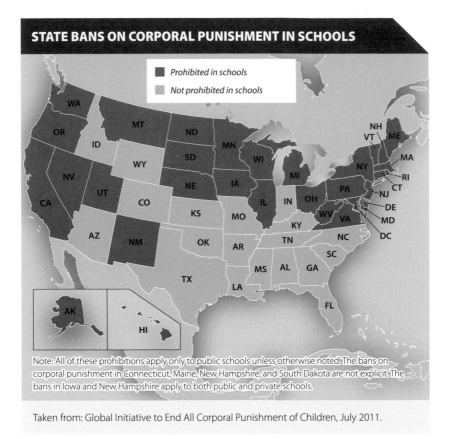

STATE BANS ON CORPORAL PUNISHMENT IN SCHOOLS

Prohibited in schools

Not prohibited in schools

Note: All of these prohibitions apply only to public schools unless otherwise noted. The bans on corporal punishment in Connecticut, Maine, New Hampshire, and South Dakota are not explicit. The bans in Iowa and New Hampshire apply to both public and private schools.

Taken from: Global Initiative to End All Corporal Punishment of Children, July 2011.

the criminal law function of government. An examination of the history of the Amendment and the decisions of this Court construing the proscription against cruel and unusual punishment confirms that it was designed to protect those convicted of crimes. We adhere to this longstanding limitation, and hold that the Eighth Amendment does not apply to the paddling of children as a means of maintaining discipline in public schools.

The history of the Eighth Amendment is well known. The text was taken, almost verbatim, from a provision of the Virginia Declaration of Rights of 1776, which in turn derived from the English Bill of Rights of 1689. The English version, adopted after the accession of William and Mary, was intended to curb the excesses of English judges under the reign of James II. Historians have viewed the English provision as a reaction either to the "Bloody Assize," the treason trials conducted by Chief Justice Jeffreys in 1685 after the abortive rebellion of the Duke of Monmouth, or to the perjury prosecution of Titus Oates in the same year. In either case, the exclusive concern of the English version was the conduct of judges in enforcing the criminal law. The original draft introduced in the House of Commons provided:

> The requiring excessive bail of persons committed in criminal cases and imposing excessive fines, and illegal punishments, to be prevented.

Although the reference to "criminal cases" was eliminated from the final draft, the preservation of a similar reference in the preamble indicates that the deletion was without substantive significance. Thus, Blackstone treated each of the provision's three prohibitions as bearing only on criminal proceedings and judgments.

The Americans who adopted the language of this part of the English Bill of Rights in framing their own State and Federal Constitutions 100 years later feared the imposition of torture and other cruel punishments not only by judges acting beyond their lawful authority, but also by legislatures engaged in making the laws by which judicial authority would be measured. Indeed, the principal concern of the American Framers appears to have been with the legislative definition of crimes and punishments. But if the American provision was intended to restrain government more broadly than its English model, the subject to which it was intended to apply—the criminal process—was the same.

At the time of its ratification, the original Constitution was criticized in the Massachusetts and Virginia Conventions for its failure to provide any protection for persons convicted of crimes. This criticism provided the impetus for inclusion of the Eighth Amendment in the Bill of Rights. When the Eighth Amendment was debated in the First Congress, it was met by the objection that the Cruel and Unusual Punishments Clause might have the effect of outlawing what were then the common criminal punishments of hanging, whipping, and earcropping. The objection was not heeded, "precisely because the legislature would otherwise have had the unfettered power to prescribe punishments for crimes." *Furman v. Georgia* [1972].

In light of this history, it is not surprising to find that every decision of this Court considering whether a punishment is "cruel and unusual" within the meaning of the Eighth and Fourteenth Amendments has dealt with a criminal punishment.

These decisions recognize that the Cruel and Unusual Punishments Clause circumscribes the criminal process in three ways: first, it limits the kinds of punishment that can be imposed on those convicted of crimes, e.g., *Estelle v. Gamble* [1976, regarding the provision of medical care while incarcerated], *Trop v. Dulles* [1958, which addressed the punishment of expatriation for desertion], second, it proscribes punishment grossly disproportionate to the severity of the crime, e.g., *Weems v. United States* [1910, in which a man was sentenced to fifteen years in a Philippine prison under harsh conditions for falsifying a document], and third, it imposes substantive limits on what can be made criminal and punished as such, e.g., *Robinson v. California* [1962, in which an individual was incarcerated in the same way as a criminal, but he was only addicted to narcotics].We have recognized the last limitation as one to be applied sparingly.

> The primary purpose of [the Cruel and Unusual Punishments Clause] has always been considered, and properly so, to be directed at the method or kind of punishment imposed for the violation of criminal statutes. . . . *Powell v. Texas.*

In the few cases where the Court has had occasion to confront claims that impositions outside the criminal process constituted cruel and unusual punishment, it has had no difficulty finding the Eighth Amendment inapplicable. . . .

Students demonstrate against corporal punishment in 1972. © Hulton-Deutsch Collection/ Corbis.

The Eighth Amendment Provides Limited Protection

Petitioners acknowledge that the original design of the Cruel and Unusual Punishments Clause was to limit criminal punishments, but urge nonetheless that the prohibition should be extended to ban the paddling of schoolchildren. Observing that the Framers of the Eighth Amendment could not have envisioned our present system of public and compulsory education, with its opportunities for noncriminal punishments, petitioners contend that extension of the prohibition against cruel punishments is necessary lest we afford greater protection to criminals than to school children. It would be anomalous, they say, if school children could be beaten without constitutional redress, while hardened criminals suffering the same beatings at the hands of their jailers might have a valid claim under the Eighth Amendment. Whatever force this logic may have in other settings, we find it an inadequate basis for wrenching the Eighth Amendment from its historical context and extending it to traditional disciplinary practices in the public schools.

The prisoner and the school child stand in wholly different circumstances, separated by the harsh facts of criminal conviction and incarceration. The prisoner's conviction entitles the State to classify him as a "criminal," and his incarceration deprives him of the freedom "to be with family and friends and to form the other enduring attachments of normal life." *Morrissey v. Brewer* (1972). Prison brutality, as the US Court of Appeals observed in this case, is

> part of the total punishment to which the individual is being subjected for his crime and, as such, is a proper subject for Eighth Amendment scrutiny.

Even so, the protection afforded by the Eighth Amendment is limited. After incarceration, only the "'unnecessary and wanton infliction of pain,'" *Estelle v. Gamble*, quoting *Gregg v. Georgia*, constitutes cruel and unusual punishment forbidden by the Eighth Amendment.

School Children Do Not Need Eighth Amendment Protection

The school child has little need for the protection of the Eighth Amendment. Though attendance may not always be voluntary, the public school remains an open institution. Except perhaps when very young, the child is not physically restrained from leaving school during school hours; and at the end of the school day, the child is invariably free to return home. Even while at school, the child brings with him the support of family and friends, and is rarely apart from teachers and other pupils who may witness and protest any instances of mistreatment.

The openness of the public school and its supervision by the community afford significant safeguards against the kinds of abuses from which the Eighth Amendment protects the prisoner. In virtually every community where corporal punishment is permitted in the schools, these safeguards are reinforced by the legal constraints of the common law. Public school teachers and administrators are privileged at common law to inflict only such corporal punishment as is reasonably necessary for the proper education and discipline of the child; any punishment going beyond the privilege may result in both civil and criminal liability. As long as the schools are open to public scrutiny, there is no reason to believe that the common law constraints will not effectively remedy and deter excesses such as those alleged in this case.

We conclude that, when public school teachers or administrators impose disciplinary corporal punishment, the Eighth Amendment is inapplicable.

> *"Corporal punishment is a destructive form of discipline that is ineffective in producing educational environments in which students can thrive."*

Corporal Punishment Should Be Banned in All Schools

Laura W. Murphy, Deborah J. Vagins, and Alison Parker

The American Civil Liberties Union (ACLU) and Human Rights Watch, two advocacy organizations dedicated to human rights in the United States and worldwide, have taken strong stances against corporal punishment. In the following viewpoint, Laura W. Murphy, Deborah J. Vagins, and Alison Parker argue that corporal punishment should be banned in all US public schools. They maintain that the practice is discriminatory because students of color and students with disabilities experience disproportionately more corporal punishment than other students. The authors say corporal punishment has been shown to have a negative impact on the educational environment and, in some cases, incites violence and anger in otherwise obedient individuals. Thus, Murphy, Vagins, and Parker advocate for a ban of the practice in public schools and for the adoption of positive behavior supports. Murphy is the direc-

Laura W. Murphy, Deborah J. Vagins, and Alison Parker, "Statement Before the House Education and Labor Subcommittee on Healthy Families and Communities, Hearing on 'Corporal Punishment in Schools and Its Effect on Academic Success,'" US House of Representatives, April 15, 2010.

tor of the ACLU Washington Legislative Office, and Vagins is the office's legal counsel. Parker is the director of the US Program at Human Rights Watch.

Each year, hundreds of thousands of students are subjected to corporal punishment in public schools. Despite the many problems associated with the hitting or paddling of students, corporal punishment is a legal form of school discipline in 20 states. Of these, thirteen states have reported that corporal punishment was inflicted on over one thousand students—and eight states reported its use against at least ten thousand students—during the 2006–2007 school year. While significant, these numbers do not tell the whole story. These statistics only reflect data which has been reported to the Department of Education and they only include the number of students who are subjected to corporal punishment during the school year, not the total number of times that an individual student has been hit over his or her educational career.

Aside from the infliction of pain and the physical injuries which often result from the use of physical punishments, these violent disciplinary methods also impact students' academic achievement and long-term well-being. Despite significant evidence that corporal punishment is detrimental to a productive learning environment, there is currently no federal prohibition on the use of physical discipline against children in public school. In fact, children in some states receive greater protections against corporal punishment in detention facilities than they do in their public schools.

Corporal Punishment Affects Minorities Disproportionately

Students of color and students with disabilities are disproportionately subjected to corporal punishment, hampering their access to a supportive learning environment. According to the Department of Education, while African Americans make up

17.1 percent of public school students nationwide, they accounted for 35.6 percent of those who were paddled during the 2006–2007 school year. In *A Violent Education* and *Impairing Education*, two joint reports published by the ACLU [American Civil Liberties Union] and HRW [Human Rights Watch] detailing the effects of corporal punishment in public schools, interviewees noted the disproportionate application of corporal punishment:

- One Mississippi high school student described the administration of corporal punishment in her school this way: "every time you walk down the hall you see a black kid getting whipped. I would say out of the whole school there's only about three white kids who have gotten paddled."

- A Mississippi teacher also noted the racial disparity in the administration of corporal punishment: "I've heard this said at my school and at other schools: 'This child should get less whips, it'll leave marks.' Students that are dark-skinned, it takes more to let their skin be bruised. Even with all black students, there is an imbalance: darker-skinned students get worse punishment. This really affected me, being a dark-skinned person myself."

Evidence shows that students with disabilities are also disproportionally subjected to corporal punishment. The Department of Education has reported that although students with disabilities constitute 13.7 percent of all public school students, they make up 18.8 percent of those who are subjected to corporal punishment. In many of these cases, students were punished for exhibiting behaviors related to their disabilities, such as autism or Tourette's syndrome. The effects of corporal punishment on students with disabilities can dramatically impact their behavior and hamper their academic performance. In *Impairing Education*, parents and grandparents of students with disabilities noted the changes in behavior and barriers to educational achievement stemming from the use of corporal punishment:

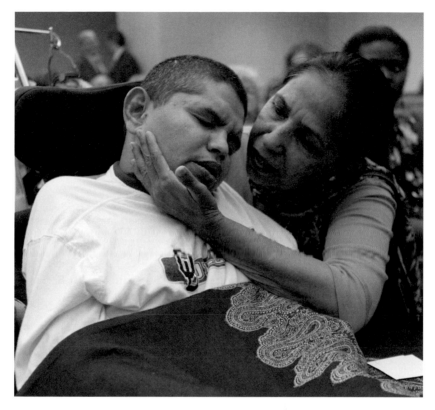

Farhat Chishty comforts her mentally handicapped child who was a victim of physical abuse by a school staff member. Students of color and students with disabilities are disproportionately subjected to corporal punishment. © AP Photo/Harry Cabluck.

- A grandmother of a student who has Asperger's syndrome withdrew him from his Oklahoma school in part because of the hostile environment stemming from frequent use of corporal punishment: "It made him much more introverted. He very much didn't want to go to school . . . No one's supposed to go to school to be tortured, school is supposed to be fun."
- A mother of a student with autism reported that her son's behavior changed after he was struck in his Florida school: "He's an avoider by nature, before he was never aggressive. Now, he struggles with anger; right after the incidents he'd have anger explosions."

Hitting any student should be an unacceptable practice, but the disproportionate application of corporal punishment further undermines the educational environment for minority groups and students with disabilities. A federal prohibition on corporal punishment in public schools is necessary to protect students from the discriminatory impact and the academic harms which it brings.

Corporal Punishment Hinders Academic Performance

Harsh physical punishments do not improve students' in-school behavior or academic performance. In fact, one recent study [by writer and activist Michael Hickman titled "Study: Paddling vs. ACT Scores and Civil Immunity Legislation"] found that in states where corporal punishment is frequently used, schools have performed worse academically than those in states that prohibit corporal punishment. While most states demonstrated improvements in their American College Testing (ACT) scores from 1994 to 2008, "as a group, states that paddled the most improved their scores the least." At the same time "the ten states with the longest histories of forbidding corporal punishment improved the most" with improvement rates three times higher than those states which reported frequent use of corporal punishment.

Many children who have been subjected to hitting, paddling or other harsh disciplinary practices have reported subsequent problems with depression, fear and anger. These students frequently withdraw from school activities and disengage academically. The Society for Adolescent Medicine has found that victims of corporal punishment often develop "deteriorating peer relationships, difficulty with concentration, lowered school achievement, antisocial behavior, intense dislike of authority, somatic complaints, a tendency for school avoidance and school drop-out, and other evidence of negative high-risk adolescent behavior." One Mississippi student interviewed for *A Violent*

Education described the effects of corporal punishment on his attitude towards school:

- "[Y]ou could get a paddling for almost anything. I hated it. It was used as a way to degrade, embarrass students . . . I said I'd never take another paddling, it's humiliating, it's degrading. Some teachers like to paddle students. Paddling causes you to lose respect for a person, stop listening to them."

Corporal punishment places parents and teachers in positions where they may have to choose between educational advancement and students' physical well-being. For instance, some parents who learn that their children are being struck at public school find themselves without recourse, unable to effectively opt-out from the practice, and unable to obtain legal or other redress when their children have been paddled against their wishes. Ultimately some parents find that the only way they can protect their children from physical harm is to withdraw them from school altogether. Similarly, teachers who work in schools where corporal punishment is administered are often reluctant to send disruptive students out of the classroom because they are afraid the students will be beaten.

Moreover, a public school's use of corporal punishment affects every student in that school, including those who are not personally subjected to hitting or paddling. The prevalent use of physical violence against students creates an overall threatening school atmosphere that impacts students' ability to perform academically. Often, children who experience or witness physical violence will themselves develop disruptive and violent behaviors, further disturbing their classmates' learning as well as their own.

Positive Behavior Supports Encourage Learning

Corporal punishment is a destructive form of discipline that is ineffective in producing educational environments in which

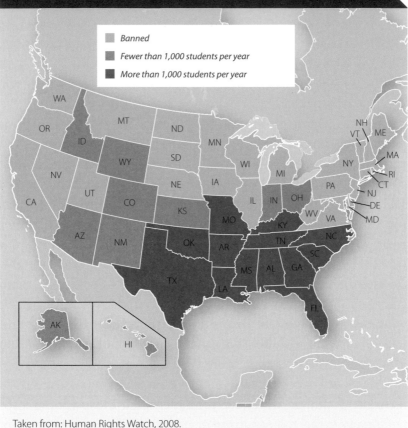

NUMBER OF STUDENTS RECEIVING CORPORAL PUNISHMENT BY STATE IN THE 2006–2007 SCHOOL YEAR

Taken from: Human Rights Watch, 2008.

students can thrive. Rather than relying on harsh and threatening disciplinary tactics, schools and teachers should be encouraged to develop positive behavior supports (PBS), which have proven effective in reducing the need for harsh discipline while supporting a safe and productive learning environment. The Positive Behavior for Safe and Effective Schools Act (H.R. 2597) would help states and Local Education Agencies (LEAs) create positive learning environments by allowing them to use Title I funds to develop PBS practices. This bill would also require the

Department of Education to provide assistance and support so that states may fully realize the potential of supportive and flexible behavior discipline practices. By abandoning ineffective and brutal disciplinary practices, and by encouraging the adoption of PBS methods, our nation can provide opportunities for all students to achieve academic success in a supportive and safe school environment. . . .

The use of violence against students is never an acceptable means of punishment—it harms students physically, psychologically and academically. The use of corporal punishment in schools is interfering with students' right to be treated with dignity and, as a result, is interfering with their right to a quality education. By prohibiting the use of corporal punishment and helping states to develop safe and effective behavioral practices, this Congress could help to ensure that our nation's children are able to achieve their full educational potential in a supportive learning environment.

> "*The school should be a safe place,
> not a place where your child gets
> injured. . . . I tried to do everything
> I could to protect my child, but that
> wasn't enough.*"

The Mother of a Student Who Was Subjected to Corporal Punishment Urges Lawmakers to Outlaw Its Use in Schools

Personal Narrative

Linda Pee

The controversy surrounding the issue of corporal punishment in schools arouses strong emotions, especially in those who have been directly impacted by the practice. In the following viewpoint, the mother of a child who experienced corporal punishment recalls her inability to protect her child from harm at the hands of her educators. Linda Pee describes the excessive bruising on her daughter's body following punishment she received at school. Pee urges lawmakers to outlaw this practice due to the physical and emotional pain it causes students and their parents.

Linda Pee, "Testimony Before the House Education and Labor Subcommittee on Healthy Families and Communities, Hearing on 'Corporal Punishment in Schools and Its Effect on Academic Success,'" US House of Representatives, April 15, 2010.

My name is Linda Pee, and I am pleased to join you today to discuss how corporal punishment had a negative effect on my daughter, Audrey, and how my efforts to protect her from the practice were unsuccessful.

I was born in Maben, Mississippi, and until July 2009, I lived in Cumberland, Mississippi. My daughter, Audrey, attended schools in the Webster County School District from second grade until twelfth grade. Audrey moved to East Webster High School in sixth grade. That first year, they sent a discipline form home with Audrey letting parents opt out of corporal punishment. You fill it out and send it back with the child, and you can tick a box saying you don't want your child hit in school. You also have to sign the handbook, stating you read the rules. I signed saying it was OK for her to be punished, because it never occurred to me she could be injured from it. I thought she would be safe in school.

An Environment of Intimidation and Fear

When Audrey was in sixth grade, she was paddled for the first time. The paddles they use look sort of like a flattened baseball bat—they're a piece of wood about 15 inches long, three inches wide, and an inch thick, with a handle at one end. The gym coach paddled her for being tardy for gym class. There were 10 kids late for class that day, and the coach lined them up and hit them on their behinds in front of the other students.

When Audrey got home that day, she was pretty upset and she told me that she had marks on her behind. When I saw the mark of the paddle, I was shocked and infuriated. I just couldn't believe it. She told me that she got one lick. I couldn't believe that one lick would make marks like that. I was so upset I called my sister, who said I needed to take her to the emergency room. So that's what I did. She had purple bruises—you could see the mark of the paddle across her buttocks.

After that incident, I made it clear to the school that I didn't want Audrey paddled again. I went in the next day and talked to

Parental Control of Punishment at School Is Limited

In *Baker v. Owen* [1975], the [US] Supreme Court affirmed the judgment of a three-judge district court panel that held school officials' deference to parental preference as to the imposition of corporal punishment on their child at school was not constitutionally required. In *Baker*, the plaintiff's parents told officials that they did not want their child spanked. Despite this request, the child was given two licks with a drawer divider that was slightly thicker than a ruler. The district court panel agreed that a parent's constitutional rights included the right to control means of discipline used upon his or her child, but that such rights were not absolute and sometimes must yield to state interests. . . .

Baker makes evident that parents asserting violations of their constitutionally based due process interests in the disciplining of their children cannot state a cause of action based on a school official's decision to inflict corporal punishment on their children, even when that punishment is severe.

Lewis M. Wasserman, "Corporal Punishment in K–12 Public School Settings: Reconsideration of Its Constitutional Dimensions Thirty Years after Ingraham v. Wright," Touro Law Review, vol. 26, no. 4, June 2011.

the principal. I made it real clear that they'd better not lay another hand on my child. And there weren't any problems for a few years.

Audrey was an OK student—she had some trouble in math— but she had no major disciplinary incidents between sixth and twelfth grade. But the atmosphere in the school—it was really one of intimidation and fear. My daughter would see children paddled all the time. She said the principal would leave the door open so people could see that he was hitting people. Some kids get upset and angry when they see their friends paddled. And some kids become used to it, as if it was just OK to see their classmates being hit. But to me, it just doesn't seem right for kids to see that in school, for them to learn that this is OK. This practice can really injure kids, it injured my daughter.

A Parent's Wishes Were Ignored

I remember, at the beginning of Audrey's twelfth grade, I got a form from the school, asking if I gave permission for corporal punishment. I was offended they had even sent the form home, I had already been so clear in my wishes. But I completed it anyway and sent it back—I put a huge "X" on the box for no paddling, and sent the form back to the school.

In March 2007, only a few months before Audrey was due to graduate, she was paddled again. She was hit for violating the dress code, because she was wearing sweatpants that fell between the knees and the ankles, in violation of a new rule stating that students could not show their ankles at school. She received two blows from the principal in his office. She was bruised again, she had bruises all over her behind. She was paddled in first period and she had bruises all over her by third period. I took her to the doctor's office and he documented the bruises, and we went to the sheriff's department.

Audrey didn't want to tell me what happened; she knew I was going to be mad. And I was mad, I was upset. I called the superintendent and told him what happened. I didn't understand how they could paddle her when I'd signed the form telling them not to. I was so upset. But the school said they couldn't find the form. I trusted the school to keep this document safe in its files.

After Audrey was paddled again, I tried everything I could think of to protect my daughter. I went to the sheriff's department, to file charges for assault. I went to a school board meeting and tried to talk about the issue, but nothing happened. I filed a case with the State Department of Education, but I got an email back saying I should go through the local body. And I tried to pursue a court case. But we couldn't get anywhere—there's immunity for teachers who paddle in school. I was left with no options. They bruised my child and injured her twice. I tried to protect her by opting her out of this horrible type of punishment, but in the end even doing that, I was unable to protect her and the school still hurt her.

Corporal Punishment Is Not the Only Option

In schools, education should be the primary focus. You want to feel like you're sending your child to a safe place. You certainly don't want your child injured and bruised. It's crazy. The school should be a safe place, not a place where your child gets injured.

What hurts most about this is that I tried to do everything I could to protect my child, but that wasn't enough. This child is a gift from God that I've vowed to protect. She's my life. I've been divorced for 13 years. When Audrey was growing up, it was me and her. It hurts that I feel like I haven't protected her. In the end, no parent should have to be worried about that.

There are other ways to change the behavior of children in school—that would have been better for Audrey. I remember when she was in elementary school she got in trouble for talking in class. I told the teacher, if you keep her in from recess and give her some extra work—that will take care of that. And it did, because social time was important to my daughter.

I don't think anybody should be hitting anybody else's children. It's not the type of decision teacher or principals should make—it's too complicated and too much can go wrong. You can't know what mood the teacher's in, whether he's mad and swings too hard. And you can't know how it'll affect a child, whether a child will be bruised or injured or worse. This just shouldn't happen in schools—not to *anyone's* child.

> "The domestic violence laws are meant
> to protect against abuse, not to punish
> parental discipline."

Domestic Violence Laws Do Not Prohibit Parents from Using Corporal Punishment as a Discipline Tool

The State Court of Appeals' Decision

Mark P. Painter

In March 2002, Matthew Adaranijo allegedly slapped and threatened additional physical violence against his daughter. At trial, he was found guilty of domestic violence; however, in the following viewpoint, Mark P. Painter, judge for the Ohio First Circuit Court of Appeals, overturns this ruling. Painter maintains that Adaranijo's actions did not inflict severe enough injury on his daughter to qualify as criminal under Ohio's domestic violence laws. In the judge's view, the appellant's actions only caused a small amount of physical harm, which he deems necessary in effective corporal punishment. The judge affirms that the state has established that it

Mark P. Painter, *State v. Adaranijo*, Ohio Court of Appeals, July 18, 2003.

will not mandate how parents discipline their children as long as no serious harm occurs.

Courts should be slow to intervene between parent and child. The criminal court is not the place to resolve petty issues of discipline. The domestic violence laws are meant to protect against abuse, not to punish parental discipline.

Defendant-appellant, Matthew Adaranijo, appeals his conviction for domestic violence. Adaranijo was accused of hitting his teen-age daughter and of threatening to "beat the shit" out of her. After a bench trial, the trial court found Adaranijo guilty. We reverse.

A Family Dispute over Punishment

One evening, Adaranijo's 13-year-old daughter, Sade, wrote a paper for school. While Sade was sleeping, Adaranijo made corrections on the paper. The next morning, March 5, 2002, while Adaranijo drove Sade to school, they reviewed the paper. Sade was not pleased with some of the changes that her father had made.

Sade testified that as she pointed out her displeasure with the revised paper, Adaranijo became angry. When she stopped reading the paper aloud, Adaranijo allegedly slapped Sade on the left side of her face and said, "[S]top contradicting this paper." He told her, "If you contradict the paper that I corrected for you one more time, I will beat the shit out of you." When she did not continue reading, Adaranijo said, "That's it," and told Sade, "I am going to take you somewhere nice and quiet and I am going to beat the shit out of you."

But Adaranijo took Sade to school, and when she hesitated to get out of the car, he hit her on the thigh to encourage her. Sade testified that she limped into school and went to the cafeteria to get some ice for her leg. She did not tell anyone what had happened. A few days later, Sade went to her mother's for the weekend. (Adaranijo had custody of Sade, and the mother had visitation privileges.) She told her mother about the inci-

PREVALENCE OF CORPORAL PUNISHMENT BY CHILD'S AGE

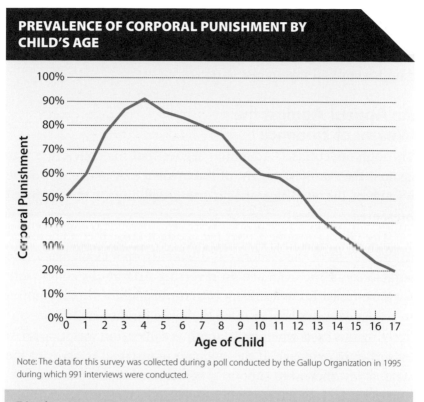

Note: The data for this survey was collected during a poll conducted by the Gallup Organization in 1995 during which 991 interviews were conducted.

Taken from: Murray A. Straus and Julie H. Stewart, "Corporal Punishment by American Parents: National Data on Prevalence, Chronicity, Severity, and Duration, in Relation to Child and Family Characteristics," *Clinical Child and Family Psychology Review*, vol. 2, no. 2, 1999.

dent. The mother immediately took Sade to a police station to file charges, but Sade refused to go in. Later, after an unrelated dispute with Adaranijo, the mother called the police and told them about the previous incident with Sade. This charge was then filed.

Adaranijo testified that on the morning of March 5, Sade was not in a good mood and was pouting. This was because he had told her that he was going to return some new clothes that he had purchased for her, due to her poor behavior. Adaranijo testified that Sade was also not pleased with the changes that he had made in the paper, but that he did not get angry. When they arrived at the school, he put the paper in her folder and tapped her on the leg with it, shooing her out of the car so that she would not be late. Adaranijo denied that he had slapped or punched his daughter or had threatened to do so. . . .

An Appeal Against the Weight of Evidence

Through his counsel, Adaranijo argues that his conviction was against the manifest weight of the evidence. A challenge to the weight of the evidence attacks the credibility of the evidence presented.

The Ohio Supreme Court has made it clear that a challenge to the weight of the evidence is distinct from a challenge to the sufficiency of the evidence. In reversing Adaranijo's conviction, we have recast his assignment of error brought through counsel to reflect what we believe to be the more fundamental issue underlying this case: whether Adaranijo's conviction was supported by sufficient evidence. If the evidence, construed in favor of the state, is insufficient to support a conviction, then no interpretation of the facts of the case will support a conviction. Therefore, if a court determines, as a matter of law, that the evidence is insufficient, the issue of whether the conviction is against the manifest weight of the evidence becomes moot.

A Parent's Punishment and Threats Are Not a Crime

In this case, Adaranijo had helped his daughter with her homework, but she was not pleased and objected to what he had done. With the facts construed in favor of the state, Adaranijo slapped Sade, threatened to beat her, and then punched her in the leg as she left the car. As to the threat to "beat the shit" out of his child—a threat he obviously did not carry out—we surmise that it was rhetorical only. Should we jail every parent for such a threat? Were these words made criminal, who would be free? Ralph Kramden [a character on the sitcom *The Honeymooners*

known for his short temper], who was never known to hit anyone, would be in jail forever.

In this case, we hold that as a matter of law, the evidence
was insufficient. There was simply no evidence to indicate that
Adaranijo's actions exceeded those within his rights under the
law of parental discipline. It does not matter whose version of the
facts we believe—even with the facts construed as most damaging to Adaranijo—he did not commit domestic violence.

Parents Are Allowed to Discipline Their Children

A parent has a fundamental liberty interest in raising and con
trolling his or her children. "Indeed, that parental right is among
those *inalienable* rights secured by natural law which Article I,
Section 1 of the Ohio Constitution was intended to protect from
infringement by the police power of the state" [as *Santosky v.
Kramer* (1982) is cited in *State of Ohio v. Hause* (1999)]. Of
course, the state has a legitimate interest in protecting children
from harm, so domestic-violence laws can apply between parent
and child. But not in this case.

The Ohio Supreme Court has held that nothing in the
domestic-violence statute prevents a parent from properly disciplining his or her child. The only prohibition [as defined in
State of Ohio v. Suchomski (1991)] is that a parent may not cause
"physical harm," which is defined as "any injury." "Injury" is defined in Black's Law Dictionary as "the invasion of any legally
protected interest of another." A child does not have any legally
protected interest that is invaded by proper and reasonable parental discipline. Thus, as any corporal punishment necessarily
involves some physical harm, the harm required to constitute
domestic violence must be greater than that here. At least one
court [in *State of Ohio v. Hause*] has held that, to rise above parental discipline and become domestic violence, the parent's act
must create "a risk of death, serious injury, or substantial pain."
None of that was present here.

An Ohio court established that the state should not intrude into the home and mandate how parents discipline their children, so long as no serious harm comes to the child. © PhotoAlto/ Sandro Di Carlo Darsa/Getty Images.

A parent may use corporal punishment as a method of discipline without violating the domestic-violence statute as long as the discipline is proper and reasonable under the circumstances. Here, there was no observable injury. We are convinced that, without observable injury, or without risk of serious physical harm, there can be no domestic-violence conviction for a parent as a result of striking a child. Though reasonable parental discipline is an affirmative defense, here the evidence not only manifestly raised the defense, it proved it. Therefore, the trial court erred in finding Adaranijo guilty.

Taking into account all the facts and circumstances in this case, we hold that the discipline administered by Adaranijo to Sade was not domestic violence. While many people differ as to whether corporal discipline should be used, it is not the business of the courts unless the child is injured. Therefore, we hold that, as a matter of law, Adaranijo's actions did not rise to a level exceeding reasonable parental discipline and, therefore, the evidence to convict Adaranijo of domestic violence was insufficient. Because the evidence was insufficient, we must reverse Adaranijo's conviction and discharge him from further prosecution.

> *"We are unwilling to establish a bright-line rule that the infliction of any pain constitutes . . . abuse, because to do so would effectively prohibit all corporal punishment of children by their parents."*

Corporal Punishment Does Not Constitute Child Abuse

The State Supreme Court's Decision

Alan C. Page

After a twelve-year-old child was paddled thirty-six times by his father on June 29, 2005, Minnesota courts were charged with the task of determining whether this act constituted child abuse. Following the incident, the father's children were removed from the home and placed in foster care. In the following viewpoint, state Supreme Court Justice Alan C. Page argues that the father's actions do not qualify as physical abuse or child abuse according to Minnesota law and thus are allowable as corporal punishment.

Minnesota Statutes § 260C.007, subd. 6, defines a "child in need of protection or services" to include a child who:

> (2)(i) has been a victim of physical or sexual abuse, (ii) resides with or has resided with a victim of domestic child abuse as

Alan C. Page, "Opinion, In the Matter of the Welfare of the Children of: N.F. and S.F., Parents," State of Minnesota Supreme Court, May 30, 2009.

defined in subdivision 5, (iii) resides with or would reside with a perpetrator of domestic child abuse or child abuse as defined in subdivision 5, or (iv) is a victim of emotional maltreatment as defined in subdivision 8.

We first address the meaning of "physical abuse" as used in subdivision 6(2)(i). . . .

Child Abuse Encompasses Many Actions

We note initially that Minn. Stat. § 260C.007, subd. 6(2), delineates two categories of children in need of protection or services: those who are themselves victims of physical abuse, sexual abuse, or emotional maltreatment; and those who are in need of protection or services only because they reside with victims of domestic child abuse or with perpetrators of domestic child abuse or child abuse. The legislature provided specific definitions of "child abuse" and "domestic child abuse" in Minn. Stat. § 260C.007, subds. 5 and 13, and it is the definition of "child abuse" upon which the court of appeals relied in interpreting "physical abuse" in this case. More particularly, the court of appeals held that (1) because malicious punishment of a child is "child abuse" under Minn. Stat. § 260C.007, subd. 6(2)(ii) and (iii), and (2) because malicious punishment of a child under Minn. Stat. § 609.377, subd. 1, requires "unreasonable force or cruel discipline that is excessive under the circumstances," then (3) "physical abuse" for purposes of Minn. Stat. § 260C.007, subd. 6(2)(i), likewise "requires unreasonable force or cruel discipline that is excessive under the circumstances."

We agree that malicious punishment of a child constitutes physical abuse that renders the child in need of protection or services. The problem is the court of appeals' holding that physical abuse "*requires* unreasonable force or cruel discipline that is excessive under the circumstances." We conclude that to limit "physical abuse" under Minn. Stat. § 260C.007, subd. 6(2)(i), to conduct that constitutes the crime of malicious punishment of a child is error.

Minnesota Supreme Court Justice Alan C. Page wrote the decision that ruled that corporal punishment does not constitute child abuse. © Anthony Barboza/Getty Images.

First, the legislature did not use "child abuse" to define children who are in need of protection or services because they have themselves been the victim of abuse or neglect. Rather, the legislature used the term "physical abuse." We presume that distinctions in language in the same context are intentional, and we apply them consistent with that intent. That the legislature did not use "child abuse"—limited as it is to specific enumerated crimes—in the context of children who have themselves been the victim of abuse or neglect indicates that the legislature intended to protect a broader range of such children. That is, the legislature intended to protect children who have been subjected to conduct constituting physical abuse, regardless of whether that conduct rises to the level of one of the criminal statutes enumerated in the definition of "child abuse" under Minn. Stat. § 260C.007, subd. 5. A broad construction of the definition of children in need of protection or services, with respect to actual victims of abuse and maltreatment, is reasonable in light of the statute's express instruction that "[t]he paramount consideration in all proceedings concerning a child alleged or found to be in need of protection or services is the health, safety, and best interests of the child."

Child Abuse Is Defined Specifically but Liberally

The legislature uses "child abuse" only in the definition of children who are in need of protection or services because of their residence—either with a victim or with a perpetrator of "child abuse." We view this as a limitation on the children who are to be adjudicated as in need of protection or services due solely to their residence, and not because they themselves have been the victim of abuse or neglect. Such a narrow construction of subdivision 6(2) is reasonable in light of the statute's express intent to remove a child from the custody of the parents "only when the child's welfare or safety cannot be adequately safeguarded without removal."

Second, while we must strictly construe criminal statutes, resolving all reasonable doubt concerning the intent of the legislature in favor of the defendant, remedial statutes are to be construed liberally. In equating "physical abuse" with the crime of malicious punishment of a child, the court of appeals necessarily adopted a strict construction of what constitutes physical abuse. A strict construction of what constitutes "physical abuse" that renders a child in need of protection or services is contrary to the liberal construction that is to be given to remedial legislation like child protection laws.

Finally, "child abuse" as defined in Minn. Stat. § 260C.007, subd. 5, includes not just malicious punishment, but also such crimes as assault of the child, use of the child in prostitution, and criminal sexual conduct. The assault or rape of a child surely constitutes "physical abuse" that renders the child in need of protection or services, even if it does not constitute "unreasonable force or cruel discipline that is excessive under the circumstances...."

Physical Abuse Includes Mental Injury

Section 626.556 defines "physical abuse" for purposes of the reporting requirement as follows:

> "Physical abuse" means any physical injury, mental injury, or threatened injury, inflicted by a person responsible for the child's care on a child other than by accidental means, or any physical or mental injury that cannot reasonably be explained by the child's history of injuries, or any aversive or deprivation procedures, or regulated interventions, that have not been authorized under section 121A.67 or 245.825.

Section 626.556 does not define "physical injury," but it does provide this definition of "mental injury":

> "Mental injury" means an injury to the psychological capacity or emotional stability of a child as evidenced by an observable

Justifying but Not Embracing Corporal Punishment

I have argued that corporal punishment is not always immoral. With appropriate restrictions and safeguards, it is sometimes permissible. . . .

Although I think that corporal punishment is sometimes justified, I nevertheless feel uncomfortable about the idea of people being punished physically. I have a distinct distaste for the practice, and in the years that I taught school children I never resorted to corporal punishment. It may seem, then, as though my moral intuitions do not match my theoretical commitments. However, I think that an unease about corporal punishment is perfectly compatible with my theoretical position. There are many unpleasant practices that, although sometimes justified, should never be gleefully embraced. For example, it is sometimes justified to take another person's life, as in the case of self-defense, yet even in these circumstances we would judge the killer to be morally defective if he enjoyed or even failed to detest his killing of the aggressor. A killing is to be regretted even when it is justified.

David Benetar, "Corporal Punishment," Social Theory and Practice, *vol. 24, no. 2, Summer 1998.*

or substantial impairment in the child's ability to function within a normal range of performance and behavior with due regard to the child's culture.

Because the definition of "physical abuse" under the reporting statute, Minn. Stat. § 626.556, subd. 2(g), expressly includes "mental injury," section 626.556 requires the reporting of the infliction of mental, as well as physical, injuries upon a child. Physical abuse may result in significant mental injury, even if it results in no observable physical injury. It would be incongruous for the legislature to require the reporting of mental injuries inflicted upon a child, yet leave the courts without jurisdiction to provide protection to such an injured child or to require that services be provided to the child's family. At the same time, the legislature's definition of "mental injury" under the reporting statute appropriately narrows the range of adverse mental effects that qualify as mental injury for these purposes: the injury must be "evidenced by an observable or substantial impairment in the child's ability to function within a normal range of performance and behavior." Minn. Stat. § 626.556, subd. 2(m). We therefore conclude that the court of appeals erred in excluding physical abuse that results in mental injury from conduct that renders a child in need of protection or services under Minn. Stat. § 260C.007, subd. 6(2)(i).

Based on the foregoing analysis, we conclude that physical abuse that causes only mental injury may nevertheless qualify as physical abuse for purposes of the definition of a child in need of protection or services under Minn. Stat. § 260C.007, subd. 6(2)(i). A child is therefore in need of protection or services under section 260C.007 if there is physical conduct toward the child that causes either physical injury, or mental injury as defined in Minn. Stat. § 626.556, subd. 2(m).

Reasonable Discipline Is Not Abuse

We next apply this definition to the stipulated facts of this case. As to whether there was physical injury to G.F., the county concedes the record is unclear. The guardian ad litem [legal guardian during litigation] urges us to find that the infliction of physical pain, even without specific injury, should be sufficient, and argues that we can infer that paddling a child 36 times inflicts pain. We are unwilling to establish a bright-line rule that the infliction of any pain constitutes either physical injury or physical abuse, because to do so would effectively prohibit all corporal punishment of children by their parents. Because the definition of "physical abuse" under the reporting statute, Minn. Stat. § 626.556, subd. 2(g), and the definition of "emotional maltreatment" under the

CHIPS [Child in Need of Help or Protection] statute, Minn. Stat. § 260C.007, subd. 15, both explicitly exclude "reasonable discipline," it is clear to us that the legislature did not intend to ban corporal punishment. Moreover, even if pain alone could be a basis on which to conclude that physical abuse has occurred, the bare-bones stipulation of facts that forms this record is an inadequate basis on which to reach such a conclusion here.

As to whether there was mental injury comprising physical abuse for purposes of Minn. Stat. § 260C.007, subd. 6(2)(i), the question is whether the stipulated facts establish by clear and convincing evidence "an injury to the psychological capacity or emotional stability of [G.F.] as evidenced by an observable or substantial impairment in [his] ability to function within a normal range of performance and behavior." G.F.'s use of the knife to make a suicide threat suggests the paddling may have had some effect on G.F.'s psychological or emotional stability. Clearly, wielding the knife in conjunction with the suicide threat raises serious concerns that must be addressed. But for there to be a mental injury and thus physical abuse there must be more. There must be a showing that the injury resulted in an "impairment in [G.F.'s] ability to function within a normal range of performance and behavior." The bare-bones record here does not support a conclusion that there was such an impairment. The record is simply silent on G.F.'s ongoing ability to function within a normal range of performance and behavior. Given this silence, we are not in a position to hold, based solely on the suicide threat involving the knife, that G.F. is in need of protection or services.

> "Sending teenagers to boot camp is often
> a decision that saves lives, and futures,
> without the scar that jail time leaves on
> their record."

Sending Teenagers
to Boot Camps

Professor's House

In the following viewpoint, Professor's House, a website that offers advice on parenting, explains why juvenile boot camps may be a good option for parents who want to correct their child's troubled behavior. The website states that boot camps are not right for all teens with behavior problems and should be considered a last resort for parents. In addition, the website stipulates that teens that get the most out of a boot camp are those whose parents make a strong commitment to a broader life-changing plan. While Professor's House acknowledges that some boot camps have been accused of abuse in their strict treatment of teens, others strive firmly but lawfully to shape young people into disciplined achievers.

With all the negative influences out there grabbing our kids today, sending teenagers to boot camps may very well be a reasonable and loving choice when teen behavior starts to erode the family bliss. Most parents and caretakers struggle with this decision the same way that they would struggle with whether to let their child spend the night in jail after their 4th DUI [driving under the influence] arrest. Sometimes loving a child means setting firm boundaries and creating scenarios that force them to learn and grow. Hopefully.

Teenage boot camps have made a name for themselves in the "tough love industry" through many successful camps that have literally kept kids out of jail and turned them back toward the college track. With a higher success rate than housing our kids in jail and other behavior modification institutions, why wouldn't a parent engage the help of a boot camp to help their struggling teen?

For the parent on the brink of packing their kid's bags, the only word of advice to offer is choose wisely. The terms "tough love" and "injury" should not go hand in hand. When checking out various camps (and you should check them out thoroughly) insist on seeing incident report summaries that indicate a true injury ratio. A high incident of injury can lead one to believe that the love received might be a little too tough. There have been cases of abusive behavior by either students or staff members reported throughout some boot camps.

Of course, a certain amount of physical risk is to be assumed. These camps are designed to push kids to their emotional and physical limits and to train them in the line art of self discipline. This may mean serious exercise sessions, overnight trail hikes, and the introduction of outdoor survival. In other cases, the student body has initiating rituals that all new inductees must go through, which usually involved physical violence. This is not a pretty aspect of the boot camp industry, but it is a reality.

Sending teenagers to boot camps is generally a last resort, saved for kids who are literally heading toward gangs, drugs, violence, and eventually death. Sending your child off to boot camp for failing math might be considered a bit harsh, especially if they have an otherwise average teenage existence. Boot camp is also not an alternative to parental involvement. Parents need

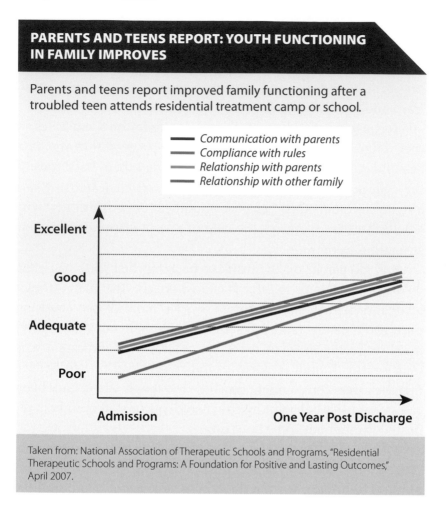

PARENTS AND TEENS REPORT: YOUTH FUNCTIONING IN FAMILY IMPROVES

Parents and teens report improved family functioning after a troubled teen attends residential treatment camp or school.

— *Communication with parents*
— *Compliance with rules*
— *Relationship with parents*
— *Relationship with other family*

Excellent

Good

Adequate

Poor

Admission   One Year Post Discharge

Taken from: National Association of Therapeutic Schools and Programs, "Residential Therapeutic Schools and Programs: A Foundation for Positive and Lasting Outcomes," April 2007.

to be sure that they have stepped up, tried various parenting methods to turn their teen's attention toward more positive influences, and have dealt with any obvious trauma before signing their child up for a camp session.

Sometimes, teenage boot camp is enforced by a juvenile judge as an alternative to a jail sentence. This is usually prescribed for special cases, first time offenders, and times when the judge feels that jail would be detrimental to any chance the child has of recovering from the situation. In such cases, parents can request that they be permitted to select the camp for the term, pending judge's approval. This is recommended for concerned parents who want to be sure that their teenager receives the best experience possible while minimizing any potential dangers that these camps may foster.

Boot camp leaders have noted that those kids who have family support, family involvement, and at least one parent who stands behind their child's success are those who end up doing well at the end of their term. Many lives have been turned around quite successfully by these programs, but generally not without a caring adult on the other side to help keep the progress going. These kids face a lot of pressure to return to their old friends and their old ways after their camp session concludes. Some kids even "owe debts" to their former gangs and friends that could be collected upon at any time. These debt collections can come in the form of some pretty gruesome attacks that no teenager wants to experience. Some kids find that even if they want to do well and apply their new knowledge after camp, the threat posed by their former associates is stronger than their will to overcome. After all, who wants to find their face slashed in the hallway in between Science class and the gym? These pressures are very real and these kids need supportive parenting when they return home.

Teenagers in boot camp and those who are coming out of camp need a plan. Kids who find themselves on the fast train to juvenile detention, jail, or boot camp didn't end up there suddenly and unexpectedly. There has been a long history of behavioral mischief that has escalated over time. Many kids start visiting the principal as early as the first grade and wind up culminating their educational career with an expulsion. Because these behaviors and problems have been developing for a period of time, parents cannot expect that there will be overnight changes in their child. Boot camp is designed to strip away what these troubled youths have been building upon. However, once you strip away a kid's issues you then have to replace it with positive involvement. For some kids, this might be nothing more than the introduction of a

Teenagers participate in a training exercise at a boot camp facility for troubled children.
© Viktor Drachev/AFP/Getty Images.

passionate endeavor. For other kids, it's going to take some time, effort, trial, error, and a lot of devotion to the plan.

So how do teenagers that have attended boot camps feel about their experience? I managed to track down three kids, between the ages of 15 and 17, who have come out of their camp experience within the last eighteen months. Two feel that they have successfully turned their life around. They feel as though they were able to take responsibility for their own future and one even stated that he didn't "need to become a statistic just because the school expects him to be one." One teen felt that boot camp was used as punishment for not being "good enough" around the house and that the punishment was unfair. On the plus side, he hasn't ditched a day of school or done any drugs since he returned home at the beginning of summer.

Boot camp is a decision that only a parent can make based on the information they have in front of them. When kids are in trouble, drastic action can be the only recourse. There are countries that require kids to spend two to four years in their national army upon their eighteenth year to help instill discipline and to teach many of the same principles. In this country, we offer our kids a choice. When kids are making dangerously poor choices, parents and caretakers need to step in and help them save themselves. Sending teenagers to boot camp is often a decision that saves lives, and futures, without the scar that jail time leaves on their record.

| *"Tough love programs are ineffective, based on pseudoscience, and rooted in a brutal ideology that produces more harm than most of the problems they are supposedly aimed at addressing."*

Teen Boot Camps Are Ineffective and Dangerous

Maia Szalavitz

Maia Szalavitz is a health journalist and the author of Help at Any Cost: How the Troubled-Teen Industry Cons Parents and Hurts Kids. *In the following viewpoint, Szalavitz argues that juvenile boot camps designed to rehabilitate delinquents are really centers of abuse and intimidation. Insisting that "tough love" approaches based on violence and humiliation are unsuccessful in reforming wayward youth, Szalavitz maintains that boot camps need to be shut down. She hopes that reported abuse of young people and the tragic deaths of several boot camp enrollees will convince lawmakers and the public that this form of juvenile detention is inhumane and ineffectual.*

The state of Florida tortured 14-year-old Martin Lee Anderson to death for trespassing. The teen had been sentenced to probation in 2005 for taking a joy ride in a Jeep Cherokee that his cousins stole from his grandmother. Later that year, he crossed the grounds of a school on his way to visit a friend, a violation of his probation. His parents were given a choice between sending him to boot camp and sending him to juvenile detention. They chose boot camp, believing, as many Americans do, that "tough love" was more likely to rehabilitate him than prison.

Less than three hours after his admission to Florida's Bay County Sheriff's Boot Camp on January 5, 2006, Anderson was no longer breathing. He was taken to a hospital, where he was declared dead early the next morning.

A video recorded by the camp shows up to 10 of the sheriff's "drill instructors" punching, kicking, slamming to the ground, and dragging the limp body of the unresisting adolescent. Anderson had reported difficulty breathing while running the last of 16 required laps on a track, a complaint that was interpreted as defiance. When he stopped breathing entirely, this too was seen as a ruse.

Ammonia was shoved in the boy's face; this tactic apparently had been used previously to shock other boys perceived as resistant into returning to exercises. The guards also applied what they called "pressure points" to Anderson's head with their hands, one of many "pain compliance" methods they had been instructed to impose on children who didn't immediately do as they were told.

All the while, a nurse in a white uniform stood by, looking bored. At one point she examined the boy with a stethoscope, then allowed the beating to continue until he was unconscious. An autopsy report issued in May—after an initial, disputed report erroneously attributed Anderson's death to a blood disorder— concluded that he had died of suffocation, due to the combined effects of ammonia and the guards' covering his mouth and nose.

An Industry Based on Abuse

Every time a child dies in a tough love program, politicians say— as Florida Gov. Jeb Bush initially did on hearing of Anderson's

TEEN DEATHS AT TROUBLED YOUTH CAMPS AND INSTITUTIONS INVESTIGATED BY THE US GOVERNMENT ACCOUNTABILITY OFFICE			
Sex/ Age	**Date of Death**	**Cause of Death**	**Case Details**
Female, 15	May 1990	Dehydration	• Showed signs of illness for 2 days, such as blurred vision, vomiting water, and frequent stumbling • Program staff thought she was faking her illness to get out of the program • Collapsed and died while hiking • Lay dead in the road for 18 hours • Program brochure advertised staff as "highly trained survival experts"
Male, 15	Sept. 2000	Internal bleeding	• Head-injury victim with behavioral challenges who refused to return to campsite • Restrained by staff and held face down in the dirt for 45 minutes • Died of a severed artery in the neck • Death ruled a homicide
Male, 14	July 2002	Hyper-thermia (high body temperature)	• Experienced difficulty while hiking and sat down, breathing heavily and moaning • Fainted and lay motionless • One staff member hid behind a tree for 10 minutes to see whether the victim was "faking it" • Staff member returned and found no pulse • Died soon afterwards

Taken from: Government Accountability Office, "Residential Treatment Programs: Concerns Regarding Abuse and Death in Certain Programs for Troubled Teens," Testimony Before the US House of Representatives Committee on Education and Labor, October 10, 2007.

death—that it is "one tragic incident" that should not be used to justify shutting such programs down. But there have now been nearly three dozen such deaths and thousands of reports of severe abuse in programs that use corporal punishment, brutal emotional attacks, isolation, and physical restraint in an attempt to reform troubled teenagers.

Tough love has become a billion-dollar industry. Several hundred programs, both public and private, use the approach. Somewhere between 10,000 and 100,000 teenagers are currently held in treatment programs based on the belief that adolescents must be broken (mentally, and often physically as well) before they can be fixed. Exact numbers are impossible to determine, because no one keeps track of the kids in these programs, most of which are privately run. The typical way to end up in a government-run program, such as the camp where Martin Lee Anderson was killed, is for a court to give you the option of going there instead of prison. The typical way to end up in a private program is to be sent there by your parents, though judges and public schools have been known to send kids to private boot camps as well. Since they offer "treatment," some of the private centers are covered by health insurance.

In the nearly five decades since the first tough love residential treatment community, Synanon, introduced the idea of attack therapy as a cure for drug abuse, hundreds of thousands of young people have undergone such "therapy." These programs have both driven and been driven by the war on drugs. Synanon, for example, was aimed at fighting heroin addiction, its draconian methods justified by appeals to parents' fears that drugs could do far worse things to their children than a little rough treatment could. The idea was that only a painful experience of "hitting bottom" could end an attachment to the pleasures of drugs.

But like the drug war itself, tough love programs are ineffective, based on pseudoscience, and rooted in a brutal ideology that produces more harm than most of the problems they are supposedly aimed at addressing. The history of tough love shows how fear consistently trumps data, selling parents and politicians on a product that hurts kids. . . .

An Ineffective Deterrent to Juvenile Delinquency

Military-style "boot camps" came into vogue in the early '90s as an alternative to juvenile prison. The media spread fears of a new generation of violent teenaged "super-predators," and this solution gained political appeal across the spectrum. Liberals liked that it wasn't prison and usually meant a shorter sentence than conventional detention; conservatives liked the lower costs, military style, and tough discipline. Soon "hoods in the woods" programs, which took kids into the wilderness and used the harsh environment, isolation, and spare rations to similar ends, also rose in popularity, as did "emotional growth" schools, which used isolation and Synanon-style confrontational groups.

Again, little evidence ever supported these programs. When the U.S. Department of Justice began studying the boot camps, it found that they were no more effective than juvenile prison. For a 1997 report to Congress, the Department funded a review of the research, which found that the boot camps were ineffective and that there was little empirical support for wilderness programs. In late 2004 the National Institutes of Health released a state-of-the-science consensus statement on dealing with juvenile violence and delinquency. It said that programs that seek to change behavior through "fear and tough treatment appear ineffective."

Unusual Advertisements for Boot Camps

But as the Martin Lee Anderson case makes clear, tough love continued to thrive. Indeed, the *New York Times* business section reported on tough teen programs as an investment opportunity last year [2006], saying the number of teenagers attending residential programs to deal with drug and behavior problems had quadrupled since 1995. Exposés of programs like . . . Florida's government-run boot camps almost always include positive anecdotes along with the accounts of abuse. As a result, for parents terrified of drugs, these stories seem to portray the programs as the only ones tough enough to "do what works." Since the media play positive anecdote against negative anecdote, often without citing the negative research data, exposés can actually serve as advertisements. The suggestion that the programs work serves to justify any abuse. In 2004, for example, *Time* quoted a father who said a tough-love program "improved his [son's] attitude and sense of responsibility," even as it reported that the family removed the child after finding some of the program's disciplinary measures too harsh.

One of the largest chains of currently operating tough love schools is known as the World Wide Association of Specialty Programs (WWASP), sometimes called the World Wide Association of Specialty Programs and Schools. . . . It took tactics from Synanon; its ideology, the language it uses, and its methods for discrediting teens' complaints are eerily similar.

Variously claiming to hold 1,200 to 2,500 teenagers and reporting 2003 revenues of $80 million, the group currently has at least eight affiliates, in Jamaica (Tranquility Bay), South Carolina (Carolina Springs Academy), Nevada (Horizon Academy), Utah (Cross Creek Programs, Majestic Ranch Academy), Georgia (Darrington Academy), Mississippi (Respect Camp), and Iowa (Midwest Academy). WWASP is a series of limited liability corporations that frequently switch corporate officers and names. This strategy is often used to limit losses from lawsuits by disgruntled customers, and until very recently, WWASP has been successful in deterring major law firms from pursuing such cases against it.

Through its public relations representative, James Wall of Freeman Wall Aiello, WWASP denies charges of abuse. But nine of its affiliates have closed following abuse allegations and government investigations. Mexico has shut down three programs since the late '90s; at one, police shot video of teenagers held in outdoor dog cages. (That program currently faces a civil suit by a boy who claims he not only was kept in a dog cage but was sexually assaulted and forced to eat vomit.) In 1998 the U.S. State Department found "credible allegations of physical abuse" at WWASP's facility in Samoa, citing "beatings, isolation, food and water deprivation, choke-holds, kicking, punching, bondage, spraying with chemical agents, forced medication, [and] verbal abuse." It called for an investigation by the local government, which resulted in the program's closure. The man who ran that program, who once admitted to [television program] "48 Hours" that teens had been bound with duct tape at the Samoa site, now operates the WWASP facility in Iowa. . . .

Killing Legislation That Would Regulate Boot Camps

In 2004 Marty Stephens, speaker of the Utah House of Representatives, used a procedural maneuver to block a vote on legislation, which backers say had more than enough support to pass, imposing stricter controls on a WWASP facility near Randolph, Utah. Six days later, he received a check from Robert Lichfield for his gubernatorial campaign. Lichfield insisted to the *Salt Lake Tribune* that "that check had nothing to do with" the bill's blockage. He added: "I'd like to use my means and resources to bless people's lives. Does that also imply influencing policy makers to make good policies that support good family values, quality education, and the things I believe in? Definitely."

Prior to 2005, Montana didn't require teen programs to let the state know they existed, let alone impose regulation. But local and national exposés led to calls for greater oversight. In the 2005 legislative session, Spring Creek Lodge registered five lobbyists and spent at least $50,000 to block a bill that would have imposed strict state rules, according to the *Missoula Independent*. The legislation died in the state House of Representatives. An al-

Gina Jones—mother of Martin Lee Anderson, who was killed at a boot camp in Florida— reacts to the news of the conviction of her son's killers. © AP Photo/Steve Cannon.

ternative bill, sponsored by Spring Creek's competitors, passed. It created a governor-appointed board with five members— three of whom represent the industry. One of the members is the "principal" of Spring Creek Lodge.

Deaths May Serve as a Wake-up Call

Thanks to the potent combination of political influence, industry and government fear-mongering, and media malpractice, tough love has so far survived its detractors. But Martin Lee Anderson's death may have marked a turning point.

The case has revealed the politics of tough love in one of its home states, and has turned a new spotlight on the data. In a departure from the usual journalistic pattern, the early coverage of the case consistently cited the research finding boot camps to be no more effective than juvenile prison, and editorials mainly called for their closure.

The movement toward "evidence-based" social policy has been growing since the early '90s, as insurers, patient advocates, and government agencies alike demanded proof that expensive policies produce demonstrable results. It also seems to have spurred at least some journalists to view scientific data as superior to anecdotes when assessing the performance of tough love programs. This has reduced the false balance in prior coverage that simply played success stories against abuse accounts. Some Florida papers even noted how the research and prior abuse scandals had led other states to shut down their government-run boot camps. They cited a Maryland scandal in which the *Baltimore Sun* photographed guards at a state-run boot camp openly beating inmates, which led that state to drop such programs. They also mentioned a similar scandal that prompted a federal investigation of Georgia's public boot camp programs, leading to their closure. Some coverage of the Anderson case noted the 1999 death of 14-year-old Gina Score at a South Dakota boot camp following forced exercise similar to that endured by Anderson, an incident that led that state to shutter its programs.

As the Florida case unfolded, political missteps dogged boot camp supporters. First, the state refused to release the videotape of the boy's beating to the media, leading to an outcry and greater media attention. Guy Tunnell, who had founded and staffed the sheriff's boot camp in which Anderson died, had gone on to head the Florida Department of Law Enforcement; as a result, he was initially in charge of investigating the death. Email messages from Tunnell—who serves on the board of the Drug Free America Foundation—showed that he supported the boot camp he was supposed to be objectively investigating, and that he had adamantly resisted releasing the video. The revelations prompted the appointment of a special prosecutor, generating yet more media attention. No criminal charges have been filed so far, but Anderson's family has filed a $40 million lawsuit against the state.

Because Anderson was African-American, some activists raised the question of racism. (Most teens killed in these programs have been white, since blacks are less likely to be able to afford the private camps and more likely to be incarcerated instead of diverted to public boot camps.) On April 19, students occupied the governor's office in an attempt to spur the arrest of the guards responsible for Anderson's death. Two days later, more than 1,500 people attended a rally at the state Capitol in Tallahassee calling for the state to shut down its boot camps. (Full disclosure: I spoke there about the dangers of the tough love approach.) The event was also aimed at keeping pressure on prosecutors to indict the guards and the nurse who didn't stop the beating. At the rally, two Florida legislators spoke in favor of legislation that would shut down the boot camps. Tunnell was forced to resign as head of the Florida Department of Law Enforcement after he mocked two men invited to speak at the rally, referring to Jesse Jackson as "Jesse James" and to Illinois Sen. Barack Obama (who ultimately did not attend the event) as "Osama bin Laden."

This series of events has placed an unusual spotlight on tough love, connecting it not with rehabilitation but with death, cronyism, and bigotry. Previous deaths haven't generated anywhere near as much activism.

To his credit, Jeb Bush recently signed into law a bill that shuts down the state's youth boot camps. The replacement programs it creates are prohibited from using physical punishment or "harmful psychological intimidation techniques," including humiliation and attempts to "psychologically break a child's will." But the kinder, gentler programs will still be run by the county sheriffs, and the regulations (which are limited to Florida, of course) do not apply to the majority of programs, which are private. Right now, children sent to private tough love programs have fewer rights than convicted prisoners. A parent can send a child to a private program where he can be held incommunicado until he turns 18, without any medical diagnosis or rationale for the treatment and without any oversight or means of appeal. . . .

And the parents who send their kids to these camps? For the most part, they are uninformed about the absence of evidence supporting tough love programs and often desperate to save their kids from drugs and delinquency. Until we figure out a better balance between the right of parents to place their kids in whatever programs they choose and the right of kids to be free from inappropriate punishment by agents of their parents or the state, the abuse will continue. The shame of it all is that we know hurting kids doesn't help them.

> *"The students' attorneys say World Wide charged families thousands in monthly tuition, but then failed to provide adequate education or therapeutic treatment programs."*

World Wide Association of Specialty Programs and Schools Sued by Ex-Students Claiming Abuse

Jennifer Dobner

In the following viewpoint, journalist Jennifer Dobner reports on a lawsuit launched by former students against a string of "behavior modification" camps and institutions. Dobner explains that more than 350 students united to complain of verbal abuse, inadequate housing, physical punishment, and other inhumane treatment at various facilities owned by the World Wide Association of Specialty Programs and Schools (WWASP). She writes that even though the case has not gone to court, authorities in the United States and abroad have already been investigating and, in certain cases, shutting down some of these camps for violating various legal codes.

SALT LAKE CITY—A Utah company that ran a network of domestic and international schools for troubled teens is being sued by more than 350 former students who claim they were denied food and medical care, lived in filth and suffered extreme physical and sexual abuse.

"Such abuses were inflicted on some children for several years," the lawsuit states. "In many instances, the abuse could be accurately described as torture of children."

Among the abuses detailed in the lawsuit include being exposed to extreme hot or cold temperatures for extended periods; being forced to eat raw or rotten foods or to eat their own vomit; being bound by the hands and feet; and being placed in isolation, including being locked inside small boxes or cages.

Some students also allege they were emotionally and verbally abused, were forced to wear unwashed clothing for weeks, were prevented from using bathrooms, were deprived of sleep and were deprived of any religious affiliations other than Mormonism.

The lawsuit was filed on behalf of more than 350 former students and 150 of their parents in Salt Lake City's 3rd District Court last week. The students are from 38 states, England and Canada and attended the residential school programs between the mid-1990s and mid-2000s.

Named as defendants in the lawsuit are the World Wide Association of Specialty Programs and Schools and its three principals, Robert B. Lichfield of Toquerville, and Brent M. Facer and Ken Kay, both of St. George.

Also named are a network of nearly 50 other affiliated businesses and individuals, which the lawsuit claims were also controlled by the organization's principals through either family relationships or written management agreements.

No hearings have been set in the case, and it was not immediately clear whether any of the 54 defendants were represented by attorneys.

The lawsuit alleges fraud, breach of contract and abuse by the World Wide Association of Specialty Programs and Schools

Being placed in isolation and inside small boxes or cages were some of the abuses committed by "behavior modification" camps and institutions. © Mika/Corbis.

and its affiliates and seeks a jury and unspecified damages. The suit renews claims in a 2006 lawsuit filed in Salt Lake City's U.S. District Court that was dismissed by a judge for jurisdictional reasons in August.

The attorneys who represented the schools, Lichfield, Facer and Kay, in that lawsuit did not immediately respond to telephone and email messages Thursday.

In court papers, attorneys for the students say World Wide has operated more than 20 schools in seven states and in Costa Rica, Jamaica, Mexico, Samoa and the Czech Republic, although the exact number and how many remain in operation is unclear.

Many of the schools were open for only short periods because of their failure to comply with licensing and regulatory laws, because of abuse allegations, and because the organization's "principals drained excessive funds off the top," court papers allege.

New schools were continually created to take in students from schools that were abruptly shut down. But the directors and staff at the new schools were often "the same incompetent and untrained" people who ran the schools that had been closed.

The students' attorneys say World Wide charged families thousands in monthly tuition, but then failed to provide adequate education or therapeutic treatment programs.

Windle Turley, a Dallas-based attorney representing the families, says state and local authorities in some places have moved to shut down or investigate the schools. In New York, the attorney general's office conducted a criminal investigation of a school near the U.S.-Canada border. Authorities in Costa Rica and Mexico also have conducted probes, Turley said.

The New York case resulted in a 2005 settlement and the school was ordered to partially reimburse tuition costs to parents and stop advertising that it offered educational diplomas because it was not recognized by the state as an accredited school, the *Deseret News* of Salt Lake City has reported.

State attorneys also said the school, Ivy Ridge, was behind one of the largest education fraud cases in New York's history.

The newspaper also reports that Mexican officials raided and shut down a school called Casa by the Sea in 2004.

How to Combat the Behavior Modification Industry

There are three approaches to minimizing the damage done by behavior modification institutes. The primary approach, of course, is to directly challenge the right of these schools to operate without tight government regulation. . . . As a second approach, we should educate our peers who are parents, or will be parents, of teenagers. . . . Parents desperate for an effective approach to reforming their children make easy prey for the misrepresentative advertising of these institutes. Finally, there is a cultural component to this fight; myths of absolute personal responsibility run deep in our nation, as does sympathy for strict discipline. Despite the mounting scientific and clinical evidence demonstrating the long-term dangers of corporal punishment, many individuals still accept the classic principle, "spare the rod, spoil the child."

Joshua Chiappelli, "Breaking Down Our Kids:
Child Abuse for Profit Is Occurring in America,"
Dissident Voice, *April 20, 2006,*
www.dissidentvoice.org.

In June, an individual student who claims he attended Casa by the Sea filed a separate federal lawsuit against World Wide and its owners.

Carl Brown Austin, 24, of Spokane, claims he spent nearly two years in the Ensenada, Mexico, school and was a "virtual prisoner" in programs that meted out primitive punishment for hours on end.

When Austin's lawsuit was filed, Facer told The Associated Press he had served on World Wide's board, but that the organization had shut down because there was no longer a need for its programs.

Asked why former students might bring such accusations, Facer said children brought to such schools have a history of misrepresenting the truth.

"That's why these kids need help," Facer said. "They lie to their parents, lie to their superiors, teachers, people who maybe they would consider an authoritative type of figure. That's not uncommon."

Organizations to Contact

The editors have compiled the following list of organizations concerned with the issues debated in this book. The descriptions are derived from materials provided by the organizations. All have publications or information available for interested readers. The list was compiled on the date of publication of the present volume; the information provided here may change. Be aware that many organizations take several weeks or longer to respond to inquiries, so allow as much time as possible.

American Civil Liberties Union (ACLU)

125 Broad Street, 18th Floor, New York, NY 10004
(212) 549-2500
website: www.aclu.org

The ACLU works to ensure that the civil rights of all Americans, especially those whose rights have been historically ignored, are observed and protected. As such, one group the organization places special focus on is youth and their rights, such as freedom of speech and due process rights in schools. In addition, the ACLU has worked on numerous national and international campaigns to ban the use of corporal punishment in schools, a practice that it views as damaging and ineffective. Reports such as *A Violent Education: Corporal Punishment of Children in US Public Schools* can be accessed on the ACLU website along with others.

American Psychological Association (APA)

750 First Street, NE, Washington, DC 20002
(800) 374-2721, (202) 336-5500
website: www.apa.org

APA is the largest scientific and professional organization of psychologists worldwide. The groups seeks to further the field of psychology by publishing new research, developing training methods, and promoting the discipline as a viable means of improving human lives and health. The organization opposes the use of corporal punishment in schools and cautions against its use in the home. Articles expanding on these positions such as "Parent's Use of Physical Punishment Increases Violent Behavior among Youth," and "Is Corporal Punishment an Effective Means of Discipline?" can be read on the APA website.

Foundation for Individual Rights in Education (FIRE)
601 Walnut Street, Suite 510, Philadelphia, PA 19106
(215) 717-3473 • fax: (215) 717-3440
e-mail: fire@thefire.org
website: www.thefire.org

FIRE was founded with the goal of ensuring that individuals' rights are preserved within the college and university setting in the United States. The organization seeks to inform the public about university policies that threaten these rights in an attempt to spur change within these institutions, focusing on four core issues: freedom of speech and expression, religious liberty and freedom of association, freedom of conscience, and due process and legal equality on campus. Information about cases being pursued by the organization as well as guides on these topics can be read on the FIRE website.

Global Initiative to End Corporal Punishment of Children
94 White Lion Street, London, N1 9PF, United Kingdom
fax: 44 (0)20 7713 0466
e-mail: info@endcorporalpunishment.org
website: www.endcorporalpunishment.org

Believing that the corporal punishment of children violates their fundamental human rights, the Global Initiative to End All Corporal Punishment of Children was formed with the goal of eradicating this practice worldwide. The organization provides extensive information regarding the negative impact of corporal punishment on children and society as a whole and has embarked on extensive international campaigns. The group's website provides research on the effects of corporal punishment as well as information about different countries' policies on this issue.

Human Rights Watch (HRW)
350 Fifth Avenue, 34th Floor, New York, NY 10118
(212) 290-4700
website: www.hrw.org

HRW is an international organization that fights for the human rights of individuals worldwide. The organization has given ongoing attention to ending corporal punishment in schools—a practice it argues is not only ineffective, but harmful to students' ability to achieve academically. Extensive information on this issue can be read on the HRW website.

National Association of School Psychologists (NASP)
4340 East West Highway, Suite 402, Bethesda, MD 20814
(301) 657-0270 • fax: (301) 657-0275
website: www.nasponline.org

NASP is an organization of school psychologists that provides professionals with resources and development opportunities to better assist students. The organization opposes the use of corporal punishment as a disciplinary method in schools and advocates the implementation of positive behavioral intervention and supports as a best practice. The organization has also investigated the use of zero tolerance policies in schools. Additional information about its views and research regarding discipline and punishment in schools can be accessed on the NASP website.

National School Safety and Security Services
PO Box 110123, Cleveland, OH 44111

(216) 251-3067

e-mail: kentrump@aol.com

website: www.schoolsecurity.org

National School Safety and Security Services is a corporation that offers school safety consulting services nationwide. The organization provides schools with an outside opinion about how to best implement individualized programs to decrease the risk of violence in schools. While the organization recognizes the problems associated with strict implementation of zero tolerance policies, it still advocates their use in a common sense manner that focuses on protecting students as a top priority.

National Youth Rights Association (NYRA)

1101 15th Street NW, Suite 200, Washington, DC 20005

(202) 835-1739

website: www.youthrights.org

NYRA is a youth-led national non-profit organization dedicated to fighting for the civil rights and liberties of young people. NYRA has members in all fifty states—more than seven thousand in total. It seeks to lower the voting age, lower the drinking age, repeal curfew laws, and protect student rights.

Southern Poverty Law Center (SPLC)

400 Washington Avenue, Montgomery, AL 36104

(334) 956-8200

website: www.splcenter.org

SPLC has been working since its founding in 1971 as an advocate and protector of the civil rights of underrepresented populations. The organization works to educate the public about civil rights issues and prosecutes cases to help ensure these rights are observed. One of the main projects of the SPLC is to reform school discipline so that at-risk children are not pushed out of the schools and into the juvenile justice system. In accordance with this goal, the center focuses on discipline methods within the schools as well as ensuring the observance of students' due process rights in the disciplinary process.

US Department of Education (ED)

400 Maryland Avenue SW, Washington, DC 20202
(800) 872-5327
website: www.ed.gov

ED is the US government agency created in 1980 to oversee the education of the nation's youth. Specifically, it has been charged with creating education funding policies and distributing those funds, conducting surveys and research to obtain current data on the schools, informing the public about current issues in the education system, and ensuring that all students have equal access to a quality education. Reports and information on a range of school discipline and punishment issues including zero tolerance policies, corporal punishment, and due process and suspension hearings can be found on the ED website.

For Further Reading

Books

Richard Arum, *Judging School Discipline: The Crisis of Moral Authority.* Cambridge, MA: Harvard University Press, 2003.

William Ayers, Bernadine Dohrn, and Rick Ayers, eds., *Zero Tolerance: Resisting the Drive for Punishment.* New York: New Press, 2001.

Ronnie Casella, *At Zero Tolerance: Punishment, Prevention, and School Violence.* New York: Peter Lang, 2001.

Philip Greven, *Spare the Child: The Religious Roots of Punishment and the Psychological Impact of Physical Abuse.* New York: Knopf, 1991.

Aaron Kupchik, *Homeroom Security: School Discipline in an Age of Fear.* New York: New York University Press, 2010.

Alice Miller, *For Your Own Good: Hidden Cruelty in Child-Rearing and the Roots of Violence.* New York: Noonday, 1990.

Brian Schoonover, *Zero Tolerance Discipline Policies: The History, Implementation, and Controversy of Zero Tolerance Policies in Student Codes of Conduct.* Bloomington, IN: iUniverse, 2009.

Russell J. Skiba and Gil G. Noam, eds., *Zero Tolerance: Can Suspension and Expulsion Keep Schools Safe?: New Directions for Youth Development.* San Francisco: Jossey-Bass, 2001.

Murray A. Straus, *Beating the Devil Out of Them: Corporal Punishment in American Families and Its Effects on Children.* Edison, NJ: Transaction, 2001.

Periodicals and Internet Sources

Paul Axelrod, "No Longer a 'Last Resort': The End of Corporal Punishment in the Schools of Toronto," *Canadian Historical Review*, June 2010.

Lisa Belkin, "When Is Spanking Child Abuse?," *New York Times*, October 21, 2008. http://parenting.blogs.nytimes.com.

Sarah Biehl, "School Expulsion: A Life Sentence?," *Children's Rights Litigation*, 2011.

Judith Browne-Dianis, "Stepping Back from Zero Tolerance," *Educational Leadership*, September 2011.

David R. Dupper, "Does the Punishment Fit the Crime? The Impact of Zero Tolerance Discipline on At-Risk Youths," *Children and Schools*, April 2010.

Maria Eftimiades, "School of Last Resort," *People*, October 23, 2006.

Deborah Fowler, "School Discipline Feeds the 'Pipeline to Prison,'" *Phi Delta Kappan*, October 2011.

Gregory K. Fritz, "Should Spanking a Child Be Unlawful?," *Brown University Child and Adolescent Behavior Letter*, November 2008.

Kim Janssen, "Under New State Law, Online Threats Can Mean School Expulsion," *Chicago Sun-Times*, January 1, 2012. www.suntimes.com.

Crystal T. Laura, "Reflections on the Racial Web of Discipline," *Monthly Review: An Independent Socialist Magazine*, July 2011.

Stephanie Martinez, "A System Gone Berserk: How Are Zero-Tolerance Policies Really Affecting Schools?," *Preventing School Failure*, Spring 2009.

Carol Marbin Miller, "Fatal Justice," *IRE Journal*, September–October 2006.

Alice Park, "The Long-Term Effects of Spanking," *Time*, May 3, 2010. www.time.com.

Teresa E. Ravenell, "Left, Left, Left, Right Left: The Search for Rights and Remedies in Juvenile Boot Camps," *Columbia Journal of Law and Social Problems*, Summer 2002.

Justin Rood, "Teen 'Boot Camps' Again in Spotlight," ABC News, April 22, 2008. http://abcnews.go.com.

Claudio Sanchez, "Texas Schools Study: Most Kids Have Been Suspended," July 19, 2011. www.npr.org.

Russell Skiba and Jeffrey Sprague, "Safety Without Suspensions," *Educational Leadership*, September 2008.

Index

A

Abandoned in the Back Row: New Lessons in Education and Delinquency Prevention (Coalition for Juvenile Justice), 64

ABC (TV network), 6

Abelow, Benjamin, 4–5

Academic performance, 12–13, 96, 98–99

ACLU (American Civil Liberties Union), 96

Adams, Lucy v. (1957), 29

Adaranijo, Matthew, 108–113

Adaranijo, Sade, 108–113

Adaranijo, State v. (2003), 8–9, 107–113

Advance Project, 68

African Americans, 95–96, 137

Alabama State Board of Education, Dixon v. (1961), 7, 20–30, *27*, 34, 41, 43

Alabama State College, 21–30

Alcohol. *See* Drugs and alcohol

American Bar Association, 68, 82

American College Testing (ACT), 98

Anderson, Martin Lee, 128–129, 131, 132, *135*, 136–137

Anger, 97, 98, 104–105

Anthony v. Syracuse University, 29

Antisocial behavior, 6, 98

Arkansas, Epperson v. (1968), 55

Armstrong, United States v. (1996), 75

Arndt, Kenneth, *74*

Arrests, 63, 64, 68, 76, 123, 137

Asperger's syndrome, 97

Assault, 17, 72, 76, 79, 87, 105, 118

Attendance, 13, 17, 52

Attention deficit disorder, 14

Austin, Carl Brown, 143–144

Autism, 96, 97

Avoidance behaviors, 44

B

Bail, 87, 89

Baker v. Owen (2011), 104

Baldwin v. Hale (1864), 55

Baltimore Sun (newspaper), 136

Barnett, United States v. (1964), 86

Barnette, West Virginia Board of Education v. (1943), 52

Bay County Sheriff's Boot Camp (FL), 129

Best interests of the child, 117

Biehl, Sarah, 60–69

Biology of Religious Behavior (Abelow), 4–5

Black's Law Dictionary, 111

Blackstone, William, 87, 89

Blackwell v. Issaquene Co. Board, 15

Board of Curators of the University of Missouri v. Horowitz (1978), 7, 42

Board of Education, Brown v. (1954), 54

Board of Regents v. Roth (1972), 51, 52, 54

Board of Trustees of University of Illinois, People ex. rel. Bluett v., 29

Boot camps
   as alternative to prison, 124, 131, 132, 136
   cages and, 134, 140, *141*
   criminal investigations of, 142

dangers, 123, 128–138
deaths, 123, 128–131, 136–137
forced medication, 134
fraud and, 142
health insurance and, 131
international programs, 133
lawsuits, 139–144
overview, 122–127
photograph, *126*
political influence and, 134–135
sexual assault and, 134
success, 126–127
tough love industry and, 123, 129, 131
verbal abuse, 134
Boyd, Local Union No. 57, etc. v. (1944), 25
Brandeis, Schaer v. (2000), 43
Brandeis University, 43–44
Brewer, Morrissey v. (1972), 55, 92
Brown, Carl, 143
Brown v. Board of Education, 54
Bush, Jeb, 129–130, 137

C
Cafeteria and Restaurant Workers Union v. McElroy (1961), 23, 24, 55
California, Robinson v. (1962), 90
Canada, 140, 142
Central Hanover Trust Co., Mullane v. (1950), 55
Child abuse, 9, 114–121, 123
CHIPS (Child in Need of Help or Protection), 120–121
Chishty, Parhat, *97*
Christie, Debbie, *63*
Christie, Zachary, 80
Coalition for Juvenile Justice, 64
Cobb v. Rector and Visitors of the University of Virginia, 34t

Codes of Conduct
Constitutional rights of students and, 18
discipline policies, 17
history, 14
legal requirements, 15–16
step programs, 16–17
Colding, Kwong Hai Chew v. (1953), 24
College. *See* Universities and colleges
Colorado, 18, 68
Columbine High School shootings, 18–19, 80
Commonwealth ex rel. Hill v. McCauley (1886), 29
Concentration, difficulty with, 98
Constantineau, Wisconsin v. (1971), 52
Convention on the Rights of the Child (United Nations), 61, 68
Corporal punishment
academic performance and, 12–13, 96, 98–99
child abuse and, 9, 114–121
circumstances and, 87
criminal offenders and, 86
criticism, 94–101
Cruel and Unusual Punishment Clause (US Constitution), 85–93
domestic violence and, 107–113
effects, 98–99
history, 11–14, 86–87
justification, 119
legality, 95
negative outcomes, 6
parents and, 6, 8–9, 102–106, 111–113, *112*
personal stories, 102–106
prevalence statistics, 95, 109

protests against, *91*
public corporal punishment, 103
purpose, 4
racial disparity, 95–98
school atmosphere and, 99, 103–105
state bans on corporal punishment in schools, 7, 9, 88
teachers and, 6, 106
See also Discipline
Costa Rica, 142
Cough drops, 82
Crime
 codes of conduct and, 14
 crime rates in public schools 2007–2008, 77*t*
 dropouts and, 64, 67
 life sentences, 61
 police involvement in schools and, 17
 school property and, 17–18
 sexual violence, 32–39, 134
 zero tolerance policies and, 76
Criminal offenders, 87–90
Cruel and Unusual Punishment Clause (US Constitution), 7, 61, 85–93
Cruel discipline, definition, 115
Cruelty, 5
Cub Scouts, 62, 80
Curwin, Richard, 16
Czech Republic, 142

D
Dannells, Michael, 45
Date rape, 35
Death, 111, 123
Delaware, 62
Depression, 98
Des Moines School Dist., Tinker v. (1969), 52

Deseret News (newspaper), 142
Detention (in school), 17
Detention facilities, 95, 125, 129, 132
 See also Prison
Dignity Denied: The Effect of "Zero Tolerance" Policies on Students' Human Rights (American Civil Liberties Union), 62
Discipline
 codes of conduct and, 17
 cruel discipline, 115
 definition, 10–11
 disciplinary systems as necessary, 31–39
 due process rights of students and, 7, 20–30
 history of school discipline, 12–14
 legalism in disciplinary codes, 40–49
 obedience and, 11
 overview, 10–19
 restorative justice and, 45
 school detention, 17
 zero tolerance effectiveness, 70–77
 See also Corporal punishment
Dismantling the School to Prison Pipeline (NAACP), 62
Dixon v. Alabama State Board of Education, 7, *27*, 34, 41, 43
Dobner, Jennifer, 139–144
Domestic violence, 107–113
Dress codes, 19, 82, 105
Dropouts (high school), 64, 67, 83
Drug crimes, 90
Drug Free America Foundation, 137
Drug sniffing dogs, 84
Drug-Free Schools and Campuses Act of 1989, 8

Drugs and alcohol
  drug free zones, *81*
  learning abilities and, 14
  legislative requirement for dis-
    cipline and, 8
  police and, 17
  random drug testing, 19
  sexual violence and, 33
  Synanon and, 131, 132
  zero tolerance policies, 8, 79, 82
Due process
  codes of conduct and, 18
  exceptions, 58
  expulsion and, 7–8, 20–30
  Fifth Amendment (US
    Constitution) and, 24
  Fourteenth Amendment (US
    Constitution) and, 7–8, 86
  fundamental rights and, 29–30
  hearings and, 7–8, 34, 41–43,
    50–59, 55
  notice and, 21, 24–26, 29, 30,
    55–59, 65, 72, 73
  parent rights regarding corporal
    punishment in schools and,
    104
  procedural requirements, 22
    public school students and, 7
  right to counsel, 34, 38
  student rights, 7, 20–30
  substantive due process, 34
  university students and, 7
  zero tolerance policies and, 72,
    76
Dulles, Trop v. (1958), 90

E
Edmonson Oil Co., Lugar v. (1982)
  28
*Education on Lockdown: The
  Schoolhouse to Jailhouse Track*
  (Advancement Project), 62

Eighth Amendment (US
  Constitution)
  criminal offenders and, 87–90
  Cruel and Unusual Punishment
    Clause, 7, 61, 85–93
  limited protection, 91–92
  purpose, 89–90
Emotional disturbance, 14
Ending the School to Jail Track
  (Padres & Jóvenes Unidos), 68
England, 5, 88–89, 140
English Bill of Rights of 1689, 88,
  89
Enlightenment, Age of, 5
Epperson v. Arkansas (1968), 55
Estelle v. Gamble (1976), 90, 92
*Ewing, Regents of the University of
  Michigan v.* (1985), 42–43
Expulsion. *See* School expulsion

F
Facer, Brent M., 140, 142–144
Farley, Laney v. (2007), 9
Fear, 98, 103–105, 132
Fifth Amendment (US
  Constitution), 24
Fines, 87, 89
First Amendment (US
  Constitution), 43, 46–47
Florida, 97, 128–129, 133, 136–138
Florida, Graham v. (2010), 61, 62,
  67
Fourteenth Amendment (US
  Constitution)
  codes of conduct and, 18
  due process and, 7–8, 86
  education rights and, 65
  hearing requirements, 7–8,
    50–59
  protections universities provide
    and, 28
Framers of US Constitution, 89, 91

Frankfurter, Felix, 22
Freeman Wall Aiello, 133
Fuentes v. Shevin (1972), 54
Furman v. Georgia (1972), 90

G
Gabrilowitz v. Newman, 34t
Gale Encyclopedia of Everyday Law, 10–19
Gamble, Estelle v. (1976), 90, 92
Gangs, 80, 125
Georgia, 18, 133, 136
Georgia, Furman v. (1972), 90
Georgia, Gregg v., 92
Gershoff, Elizabeth, 6
Gleason v. University of Minnesota (1908), 29
Goodreau v. Rector and Visitors of the University of Virginia, 34t
Goss v. Lopez (1975), 7, 50–59, 65
Graham v. Florida (2010), 61, 62, 67
Grannis v. Ordean (1914), 55
Gregg v. Georgia, 92
Gun Free Schools Act of 1994, 8, 80
Guns and weapons
    imaginary guns, 80, 81
    mandatory expulsion and, 8
    police involvement and, 17
    toy guns, 79
    zero tolerance policies, 18–19, 79

H
Hale, Baldwin v. (1864), 55
Harper, F., 87
Harvard University, 29
Hate speech, 46–47
Hause, State of Ohio v. (1999), 111
Hearings
    court proceedings and, 58–59
    due process, 7–8, 34, 41–43, 50–59, 55

school expulsions and, 7–8, 41–43, 50–59
suspension and, 66
See also Due process
Herbert, Bob, 65
Hickman, Michael, 98
Honor codes, 46
Horowitz, Board of Curators, University of Missouri v. (1978), 7, 42
Houston, Irene, 64
HRW (Human Rights Watch), 96
Hyperactivity, 14

I
Illinois, 13, 71
Impairing Education (ACLU & HRW), 96
In loco parentis, 6, 13, 28
In the Matter of the Welfare of the Children of N.F. and S.F., Parents (2007), 9
Indicators of School Crime and Safety (National Center for Educational Statistics), 73
Ingraham v. Wright (1977), 7, 11, 85–93, 104
Injury, definition, 111
Insight on the News (website), 4
Iowa, 133, 134
Issaquene Co. Board, Blackwell v., 15

J
Jackson, Jesse, 137
Jamaica, 133, 142
James, F., 87
James II, king of England, 88
Jaska v. Regents of the University of Michigan, 34t
Joint Anti-Fascist Refugee Committee v. McGrath (1951), 22, 57

Jones, Gina, *135*
Journal of Counseling and Development, 64
Just cause (legal concept), 18
Juvenile detention, 95, 125, 129, 132

K
Kay, Ken, 140, 142
Kramer, Santosky v. (1982), 111
Kwong Hai Chew v. Colding (1953), 24

L
Lake, Peter F., 40–49
Laney v. Farley (2007), 9
Law of Torts (Harper and James), 87
Lichfield, Robert, 134, 140, 142
Life sentences, 61
Lipstick, 82
Local Union No. 57, etc. v. Boyd (1944), 25
Lockdowns, 84
Locke, John, 5
Lopez, Goss v. (1975), 7, 50–59,65
Lowery, John Wesley, 45
Lucy, Autherine, 29
Lucy v. Adams (1957), 29
Lugar v. Edmonson Oil Co. (1982), 28

M
Malicious punishment, 115
Mandatory education, 13, 52, 86, 91, 92
Maryland, 76, 136
Massachusetts, 7, 12, 43, 44, 89
Master academic plans (MAPs), 47–48
McCauley, Commonwealth ex rel. Hill v. (1886), 29
McElroy, Cafeteria and Restaurant Workers Union v. (1961), 23, 24, 55

McGrath, Joint Anti-Fascist Refugee Committee v. (1951), 22, 57
Medical and Surgical Society of Montgomery County v. Weatherly, 25
Medical care, 90, 140
Mental injury, definition, 118–119
Mentors, *42*, 46, 47–48
Metal detectors, 84
Mexico, 133–134, 142, 143
Mikel, Andrew, 79, 82
Minnesota, 114–121
Minnesota State Supreme Court, 9, 114–121
Mississippi, 96, 98–99, 103, 133
Missoula Independent (newspaper), 134
Morales, David, 79
Mormonism, 140
Morrissey v. Brewer (1972), 55, 92
Mouthwash, 82
Mullane v. Central Hanover Trust Co. (1950), 55
Murphy, Laura W., 94–101

N
NAACP Legal Defense and Education Fund, 62
National Association of School Psychologists, 83
National Center for Education Statistics, 64, 73
National Institutes of Health, 132
National Resolution for Ending School Pushout (Dignity in Schools Campaign), 65
National School Boards Association, 70–77
Naval Gun Factory, 23
Nevada, 133
New Jersey, 7, 79, 81

New Mexico, 9

New York, 63, 142

New York Times (newspaper), 32, 65, 132

Newman, Gabrilowitz v., 34t

No-cell-phone policies, 80

Notice (due process), 21, 24–26, 29, 30, 34, 55–59, 65, 72, 73

O

Obama, Barack, 137

Obedience, 11, 84

Ohio First Circuit Court of Appeals, 107–113

Oklahoma, 18, 80, 97

Ordean, Grannis v. (1914), 55

Original Sin, 11

Owen, Baker v., 104

P

Padres & Jóvenes Unidos, 68

Page, Alan C., 114–121, *116*

Painter, Mark P., 107–113

Parker, Alison, 94–101

Parker, Francis, 13

Parson, Michael, 83

Pee, Audrey, 103–106

Pee, Linda, 102–106

Peer relationships, 98

People ex rel. Bluett v. Board of Trustees of University of Illinois, 29

Physical abuse, 118–120

Police state, 83, 84

Positive Behavior for Safe and Effective Schools Act, 100

Positive behavior supports (PBS), 99–101

Powell, Lewis F., 85–93

Powell v. Texas (1968), 86, 90

Predictors of Categorical At-Risk High School Dropouts (Suh, Suh, and Houston), 64

Prison
boot camp as alternative, 124, 131, 132, 136
high school dropouts and, 64
US Supreme Court and juvenile prison sentences, 61, 67
See also Detention facilities

Privacy rights, 18

Private universities, 29

Psychological Bulletin (journal), 6

Psychological evaluations, 72, 83

Public assistance, 64

Puritans, 11

Q

Quincy Movement, 13

R

Racial discrimination claims, 66, 75

Rector and Visitors of the University of Virginia, Cobb v., 34t

Rector and Visitors of the University of Virginia, Goodreau v., 34t

Rector and Visitors of the University of Virginia, Tigrett v., 34t

Reform school, 80

Regents of the University of Michigan, Jaska v., 34t

Regents of the University of Michigan v. Ewing (1985), 42–43

Religion, 4–5, 11

Reputation, 52, 54

Resolution Concerning School Discipline (American Bar Association), 68

Restorative justice, 45

Rhode Island, 79

Right to counsel, 34, 38

Right to privacy, 18

Robinson v. California (1962), 90

Rodriguez, San Antonio Indep. Sch. Dist. v. (1973), 65

Roper v. Simmons (2005), 61–62
Rosary beads, 80
Roth, Board of Regents v. (1972), 51, 52, 54

S
Salt Lake Tribune (newspaper), 134
Salvation, 5
Samoa, 134, 142
San Antonio Indep. Sch. Dist. v. Rodriguez (1973), 65
San Francisco State University, 16
Santosky v. Kramer, 111
Satan, 11
Schaer v. Brandeis, 43
School boards, 14, 71–77, 79, 80, 105
School expulsion
    academic performance and, 8
    due process and, 7–8, 20–30
    effects on students, 60–69
    guns and weapons and, 8, 19
    hearings and, 7–8, 41–43, 50–59
    prevalence rates, 62–64
    zero tolerance policies and, 62–63, 79
School security measures, 15*t*
School suspension
    big-city suspensions by district in 2008, 56*t*
    due process and, 9, 55
    guns and weapons and, 19
    hearings and, 66
    prevalence rates, 62–64
    race/ethnicity and, 66
    zero tolerance policies and, 62, 79, 82, 83
Score, Gina, 136
Seavey, Warren A., 29
Sexual activity, 64
Sexual misconduct, 43–44

Sexual violence, 32–39, 134
Shaughnessy, United States ex rel. Knauff v. (1950), 23
Shevin, Fuentes v. (1972), 54
Simmons, Roper v. (2005), 61–62
Smoking and tobacco, 73
Society for Adolescent Medicine, 98
Some Thoughts Concerning Education (Locke), 5
South Carolina, 133
South Dakota, 136
Spanking, 6, 7, 11
    See also Corporal punishment
Spock, Benjamin, 13
Spotsylvania High School (Virginia), 79
Spring Creek Lodge, 134–135
St. John's University, 39
State of Ohio v. Hause (1999), 111
State of Ohio v. Suchomski (1991), 111
State v. Adaranijo (2003), 8, 107–113
Steinbach, Sheldon E., 31–39
Step programs, 16–17
Stephens, Marty, 134
Stoner, Edward N., 31–39
Strickland, Wood v. (1975), 71
Strip searches, 84
Study: Paddling v. ACT Scores and Civil Immunity Legislation (Hickman), 98
Substantive due process, 34
Suchomski, State of Ohio v. (1991), 111
Suh, Jingyo, 64
Suh, Suhyun, 64
Suicide, 121
Surveillance cameras, 84
Synanon, 131, 132

Syracuse University, Anthony v., 29
Szalavitz, Maia, 128–138

T
Tardiness, 17, 103
Texas, 76, 81
Texas, Powell v. (1968), 86, 90
Tigrett v. Rector and Visitors of the University of Virginia, 34t
Time (magazine), 82, 133
Timoney, Patrick, 79
Tinker v. Des Moines School Dist. (1969), 52
Tobacco and smoking, 73
Totalitarian society, 84
Tough love industry, 123, 129, 131
  See also Boot camps
Tourette's syndrome, 96
Toy guns, 79
Trop v. Dulles (1958), 90
Tunnell, Guy, 136–137
Turley, Windle, 142

U
Unemployment, 67
United Nations Convention on the Rights of the Child, 61, 68
United States, Weems v. (1910), 90
Unites States ex rel. Knauff v. Shaughnessy (1950), 23
United States v. Armstrong (1996), 75
United States v. Barnett (1964), 86
Universities and colleges
  disciplinary systems as necessary, 31–39
  due process rights of students, 7, 20–30
  legalism in disciplinary codes, 40–49
  private universities, 29
University of Alabama, 29

University of Minnesota, Gleason v. (1908), 29
US Congress, 9, 24, 80, 101, 102–106, 132
US Constitution, 12, 89, 91
  See also specific Amendments
US Department of Education, 8, 95, 96, 100
US Department of Justice, 132
US Fifth Circuit Court of Appeals, 20–30
US House Committee on Education and Labor, 9
US Sixth Circuit Court, 9
US Supreme Court
  establishment of racial discrimination case, 75
  Goss v. Lopez (1975), opinion, 50–59
  Ingraham v. Wright (1977) opinion, 85–93
  juvenile prison sentences, 61, 67
  parents rights regards corporal punishment, 7, 11, 104
  school policies and, 71
  university discipline codes, 41
  university student due process rights, 7
Utah, 133, 134, 140

V
Vagins, Deborah J., 94–101
Verbal abuse, 134
Victorian era, 5–6
Violence
  crime rates in public schools 2007–2008, 77t
  police involvement and, 17
  sexual violence, 32–39
  zero-tolerance policies, 8, 72–73
A Violent Education (ACLU & HRW), 96, 98–99

Virginia, 79, 88, 89
Virginia Declaration of Rights of
    1776, 88
Virginia Polytechnic Institute and
    State University, 32, *37*
Von Fellenberg, Philipp Emanual,
    12–13

W
Wall, James, 133
Weapons. *See* Guns and weapons
*Weatherly, Medical and Surgical
    Society of Montgomery County
    v.*, 25
Weems v. United States (1910), 90
*West Virginia Board of Education v.
    Barnette* (1943), 52
White, Byron, 50–59, *53*
Whitehead, John W., 78–84
Willfulness, in children, 4–5
William and Mary, king and queen
    of England, 88
Williams, Walter E., 4
Wisconsin v. Constantineau (1971),
    52
Wood v. Strickland (1975), 71
World Wide Association of
    Specialty Programs (WWASP),
    133–135, 139–144

Wright, Ingraham v. (1977), 7, 11,
    85–93, 104

Z
Zero tolerance policies
    arrest and, 79
    Columbine school shootings
        and, 80
    criminalization of children and,
        78–84
    drugs and alcohol, 8, 79, 80
    effectiveness, 70–77
    equal application, 73, 75
    guns and weapons, 8, 79
    homework assignments and, 81
    legislation and, 8
    no-cell-phone policies, 80
    prosecution and, 80, 81
    reaction to social changes, 14
    rosary beads, 80
    school expulsion and suspen-
        sion and, 62–63, 79
    student awareness of legal rights
        and, 83
    student intentions and, 82
    violence, 8, 72–73